I GOT THIS

To Gold and Beyond

LAURIE HERNANDEZ

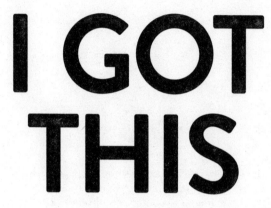

I GOT THIS

To Gold and Beyond

HARPER
An Imprint of HarperCollinsPublishers

Glossary of gymnastics terms on pages 219–26
courtesy of USA Gymnastics
Emojis © bontom / Shutterstock

ISBN 978-0-06-267731-0

16 17 18 19 20   PC/LSCH   10 9 8 7 6 5 4 3 2 1
❖
First Edition

For my grandmother Bruny; my parents, Wanda and Anthony; and my siblings, Jelysa and Marcus: I couldn't have asked for a more loving or supportive family. Thank you for always being there, in the trying times as well as in the joyous ones.

CONTENTS

INTRODUCTION

ON AUGUST 15, 2016, I WHISPERED SOMETHING TO myself that ended up being heard all around the world. *I got this*, I said as I touched the balance beam before performing my final routine in the team competition during the Summer Olympics in Rio de Janeiro, Brazil. I didn't expect those three little words to blow up on social media the way that they did—they were simply a reminder to myself that I had practiced so incredibly hard for that moment, that I could do it. I said those words to keep myself calm and focused. I said them to give myself confidence. Even months later they continued to have power for me as I competed for the Mirror Ball Trophy alongside my *Dancing with the Stars* partner, Val Chmerkovskiy. And I still say them today whenever there's a big challenge ahead.

The year 2016 was a magical one for me. So many of my wishes were fulfilled, I almost can't believe it. I recently got a journal to start committing my memories to paper, and sometimes after completing an entry I have to sit silently for a while and just absorb it all. Thinking about the Olympics still gives me butterflies! My family, my coach, and all my life experiences have taught me to pursue my goals, to never let doubt hold me back, to take the first step . . . and then the next. And that advice has paid off a thousand times over. As you read these pages, I hope you'll see that I had a dream, and that by dedicating everything I had to it, I was able to achieve it. I believe wonderful things can happen for you, too. Don't let your fears stop you. There will be setbacks and disappointments—there always are—but there will also be lots of rewards.

By sharing my story in this book, I want to encourage and dare you to go after *your* goals. I want to inspire you to do something you never thought was possible. You'll be amazed at how, by some grace, the path will clear for you. The message I gave myself on that life-changing summer day may have been "I got this," but the message I hope you hear in every line of this book is "*You* got this."

Laurie H ♡

FAMILY FIRST

CHAPTER 1

MOST PEOPLE DON'T KNOW THIS ABOUT ME, BUT the name on my birth certificate is *Lauren* Zoe Hernandez. I guess a lot of other parents in 2000 gave their daughters the name Lauren, too: there were so many of us in my first gymnastics class, my teacher decided to call me Laurie so we'd know which one of us she was talking to. From there, the nickname just kind of stuck, and now that's how I'm known. Since then I've also earned the nickname "the Human Emoji" because of the animated faces I make during my floor routines. I love the hilarious pictures of me online making the "openmouthed smiley face" and the "blushing face." There's also the "flirty face"

7

and the "scream." But the one people think most resembles me is the "epic grin." I'm definitely a happy, bubbly person, and I like the fact that it shows on my face!

A lot of the joy people see in me comes from doing what I'm passionate about, and it also comes from my home life. Before I ever learned the basics of gymnastics—how to cast well on the uneven bars, how to do a handspring on the vault—I learned the importance of being part of a loving family. My dad, Anthony Hernandez, is a court clerk for the New York City Supreme Court, and my mom, Wanda Hernandez, is an elementary school social worker. They're really adorable. My dad told me that they first met in college and that my mom would study a lot in the library (which doesn't surprise me) and my dad would always joke around with her. That's so like him—he's the comedian in the family, the one who makes us laugh all the time at the dinner table. I guess their relationship just sprouted from there. Since the beginning, communication was important to them, and they've made sure it's important to the rest of the family, too.

Because my mom grew up in a not-so-good neighborhood in New York City, where she saw a lot of verbal and physical abuse, she and my dad decided that when they raised a family, they wanted to be as far from that kind of influence as possible. As soon as they could, they moved to Old Bridge Township, New Jersey. It's a friendly community where I've lived my entire life. My mom swore to my dad and to herself that we'd never have the type of bad behavior in our home that she was exposed to as a child. She made sure that we grew up with a lot of respect and love. She had witnessed the ugly side of life and wanted to create something better for us. I know that's why my siblings and I have such an awesome connection.

Speaking of my siblings . . . my sister, Jelysa, my brother, Marcus, and I all think our parents are the best life coaches ever. They raised the three of us to treat one another with respect, and it's because of their example that we're always nice to each other. When we're walking down the street, everyone thinks it's unbelievable how calm and how playful we are together. I know it sounds strange, but we never fight, because we understand we're going to be with each other for the rest of our lives. People say, "Wait, what? You really don't fight?" And it's true, we don't. If we're upset with each other, we talk it out. You don't have to fight and ignore each other for days—that's just not something that we do in our house. And once we settle a disagreement, we leave it behind us. Our parents taught us to respect our siblings first and to always remember to show that we care.

Jay—that's what we call Jelysa—is eleven years older than me. She's more than a big sister, she's like an extra mom and one of my best friends all rolled into one. She has a master's degree and is a social worker just like my mother. Even though there's such a big age gap between us, we're really close. I know I can tell her anything, and I trust her completely. When I was younger, we used to have sleepovers in her room: I'd crawl into her bed and we'd stay up all night talking. And now that we're older, it's funny how we finish each other's sentences and how we have the same mannerisms. Sometimes it freaks people out. Like one time we were in Starbucks and we ordered cake pops separately, and without even realizing it, we said the same thing in the same exact way. The barista laughed and told us that what we'd said and how we'd said it was so identical, it sounded scripted!

Marcus is awesome, too. He's four years older than me and in college now. He's studying economics and sports management at Rutgers University in New Jersey. He's a great athlete and ran track at Old Bridge High School and was a middle-distance competitor during his freshman year of college. He participated in the NCAA Division I All-American competition, too, which is a big deal. I'm always amazed by how he did all that when there was a ton going on in his life. I've been able to really concentrate on my gymnastics, whereas he was competing and juggling so much at once: school, family, social responsibilities, track. Even when you're talented, every sport is hard and requires a lot of your attention. Right now Marcus is focusing on his studies and his work, but he still always makes time for me and is one of my biggest fans. Like, during the Olympics, he got all of Old Bridge tweeting their support for me! He says he's super proud of me, and I'm just as proud of him.

Now that I'm on the road touring and training and competing a lot of the time, I miss our family movie nights and the silly things the five of us do when we're together. I especially miss the way we crank up the music and end up spontaneously dancing when we're actually supposed to be cleaning the house. . . . Our home is crazy that way. It's always filled with laughter. Being raised in that loving, joyous environment taught me to be respectful of other people. And seeing my parents' journey, and all they've given to my siblings and me, taught me something I will carry with me for the rest of my life: you can always change your circumstances in life if you put your mind to it.

THE KARATE
KIDS

CHAPTER 2

IN ADDITION TO MY BROTHER, MY WHOLE FAMILY is actually pretty athletic. I've seen pictures of my dad playing baseball when he was younger; he was a center fielder. My mom was into volleyball and tennis and was in amazing physical condition when she was in the US Army Reserve during the 1980s. It was wild growing up and hearing all her stories about basic training. But my parents' appreciation for sports and fitness wasn't the only reason they started taking us to martial arts classes when I was just two and a half: my mom also really wanted her very own Karate Kids! Because she'd grown up in a tough environment, she was determined to teach all of us self-defense.

Although my mom only enrolled Jelysa and Marcus in the actual classes, she brought me along to the dojo to watch. She even dressed me in my own gi. Whenever my mom tells the story, she says I used to stand behind whichever sensei was teaching that day and copy every move he or she made to a T. When the senseis saw that I could keep up, they began to come over and encourage me to try different moves.

Once my mother realized just how flexible I was, she decided to enroll me in ballet classes. But at that age, all I wanted to do was dance around, and ballet was a little too serious. They did give out sugar cookies at the end of each session, so at the very least I always made sure I got through the workout—I really wanted those cookies. I must have liked the performance aspect of ballet, though, because my mom tells this story about how I shined in my first recital. We were set to perform "Animal Crackers in My Soup" at a local vocational school whose auditorium could seat about six hundred people. When the curtains parted, all the other kids hung back and some even began crying. But not me! I stepped out, found the spotlight, and did my dance exactly as we'd rehearsed. It was clear that performance was my calling.

By the time I was five years old, I was ridiculously energetic, walking around the house on my hands and constantly jumping up and down on my bed. That's when my mother decided to sign me up for acrobatics. I was so excited! But when we showed up for the first class, we found out that nobody else had registered, so the instructors were canceling it. I was devastated: I had really wanted to take that class.

Then one day I was watching TV, and I saw Shawn Johnson doing flips. I can still remember how graceful and controlled she was—even at that age I could see she was pure magic on the beam. I pointed at the screen and said, "Mom, look! I want to do gymnastics, and I want to go to the Olympics just like her!" Can you believe it? My mom could tell I was serious, so she said, "If this is what you want, I'll search for a class." And she did. That's when we found my very first instructor and signed me up for a forty-five-minute recreational class focused on the basics.

On the first day, my mom said to the instructor: "I would like my daughter to learn how to do a cartwheel and a split. If she can do that in six weeks, I'll keep her in." As you probably guessed, I learned both in less time than that. I loved flipping and watching everyone around me flipping, too. I knew right away that this was my sport. That was the end of dancing and karate lessons—I was hooked on gymnastics. One of my earliest memories of that time, right at the very beginning of my gymnastics journey, was performing in a pretend competition my instructor organized. I remember I was wearing this yellow T-shirt and it was the smallest audience ever. But, no surprise, my whole family was there. Looking at my parents in the bleachers, I kept thinking, *Hey, look at what I can do!* I was so happy.

There I was, walking on the beam, holding someone's hand in this mini pretend competition one minute . . . and then the next thing I know I'm in real competitions. The transition happened like *that.* Looking back at those early years, I think my mother got more than she ever imagined: Jelysa earned her black belt and became the Karate Kid my mom always wanted; Marcus's training in track and field guaranteed he had enough speed and stamina to run from trouble if he ever encountered it; and I was constantly in motion, beginning my path to Olympic gold and silver.

DOING MY
LEVEL BEST

CHAPTER 3

IN AMERICA, IF YOU WANT TO PARTICIPATE IN organized gymnastics and compete against other kids at your skill level, there are a few ways you can go about it. One way is to join a league like the AAU, which is a multisport organization for amateur athletes. But if you're someone like me—someone who's always dreamed of competing on the world stage—then you definitely want to participate in the USA Gymnastics program. USAG basically trains and selects up-and-coming gymnasts for the Olympics and the World Championships.

To climb the ranks of the USAG system, you have to complete ten specific training levels. Levels 1–3 teach very basic skills—that's what I was learning when I was in my introductory class. When you want to move up to the big-girl levels and start to compete, it's up to your coach to recommend you. I don't know if my first instructor thought I was talented enough or if she just saw me as a sweet kid eager to take the next step, but after being with her for a while, she told my current coach, Maggie Haney, about me.

I was seven years old when my parents and I first met Maggie. She was coaching a team of female gymnasts who were all competing at Level 4 and above. By Level 4, you need to learn a specific routine for each event, and you need to do it exactly as it's supposed to be performed. It's all about acquiring a particular skill set. Then, to advance from Level 4 to Level 5, you must achieve a certain mobility score. At first, it wasn't clear if I would fit in with Maggie's Level 4s: most of the other girls were a year or two older than me. But I was the type of student who picked up new skills quickly! After succeeding at Level 4, I stayed with the same group of girls through Levels 5 and 6. During that time, my mother, who came to see all my events, noticed that my "lines"—meaning the straight lines created by my arms and legs—were improving significantly and that my skills were developing at a more rapid pace than the other girls'. That's when we questioned whether things were advancing too slowly for me. Maggie had never trained an elite-level athlete before and therefore had no one to compare me to, so she decided it was time to contact USA Gymnastics about their Talent Opportunity Program (TOPs).

The point of TOPs is to evaluate young female gymnasts' talents. It's a combo talent search and educational program for girls between seven and ten, who are evaluated at the state or regional level. Then select athletes are invited to participate in the National TOPs test, where you're evaluated on physical abilities and some basic gymnastics skills, and you're graded based on how everyone else your age is performing. The highest-scoring gymnasts are then invited to participate in the National TOPs Training Camp.

I was only nine when I arrived at TOPs, and I had no idea what to expect. That was the first time I thought, *Wow, I'm really progressing.* I could see how far I'd come. There were all these different tests: there's a specific rope-climbing exercise you have to do, keeping your legs parallel to the floor. They also have a test where they see how long you can hold a handstand. Then there's a press-handstand test and a leg-lift test. Finally, to assess your flexibility, you have to do a series of kicks and holds.

Sure enough, after I completed the program over the course of a few days, we found out *I had gotten the number one score among nine-year-olds in the country!*

Once my TOPs scores proved my potential, training at the TOPs developmental camp was the next logical step. If you rank at the top of your age bracket in the country, you're invited to go to Karolyi Ranch in Texas. Which meant I was headed for Texas! There, I could continue learning and perfecting my skills. This camp is a rung below the camp you attend when you're training for the Nationals—which is an elite-level competition—and it shares the ranch with the national training center for the US women's gymnastics team. It was all very exciting but nerve-racking, too! At the time, the camp was run by Marta Karolyi, who had been the USA National Team coordinator since 2001. Marta is legendary for having helped mold some of the greatest gymnasts in the world. It was a real privilege to be able to go there.

The camp is on this huge complex in Huntsville, Texas. It has state-of-the-art equipment, a dance room, several different types of gyms, a medical room, a dining hall, and dorm rooms. In the beginning I was training there for five days every two months; later, I would train there for five days every month. Marta brought in experts to give us tips and to help our coaches learn different techniques, too. I'd study new skills and then go home to New Jersey and work on them with Maggie at Monmouth Gymnastics Academy until I returned again the next month to show the camp staff my progress. I loved those weeks at the camp, and it was there that I realized I wanted to dedicate myself to gymnastics full-time.

All the gymnasts had practice sessions in the morning and afternoon, and we had lots of fun in between, too. I met girls from everywhere in the country, and we slept in bunk beds in dorms that looked like log cabins. In Huntsville I was also surrounded by nature, and I encountered so many different types of animals. It's where I saw my first armadillo! I felt like I was growing by leaps and bounds, inside and out—just like a gymnast is supposed to.

That's also when homeschooling began. It became necessary because I was traveling so much between home and Texas. People often ask me if it was hard leaving my New Jersey classmates behind, but what they don't realize is that I started homeschooling when I was only two weeks into third grade. So it wasn't as if I was leaving lifelong friends. Not to mention that I was in the gym all day, doing what I loved most! And there were still lots of kids in my neighborhood in New Jersey I enjoyed playing with. Our community was unusually close, and each year we celebrated major holidays with the same group of family friends. My favorite get-together was our annual New Year's Eve party, where we'd have a formal dinner with lots of music. It wasn't only the parents who got up to dance—all the kids would be twirling around and having a ball, too. And then there were my best friends, Shannon and Paloma Rodriguez, who are like sisters to me. My mom and their mom, Anna, met in the military and became super close. By some crazy coincidence, my mom also knew their father, Juan, when the two of them were growing up in New York. Anna and Juan are literally my parents' best friends in the world. They're Marcus's godparents, and my mom and dad are both Shannon's and Paloma's godparents. They live nearby, too, so we see them all the time—we've even vacationed together. That's how much like a tight-knit family we are! So between Shannon and Paloma, all my cool neighbors, and my gym friends, I was never lonely.

And, to tell you the truth, I actually liked home-schooling. The particular distance-learning program I used is called A Beka Academy. It's a Christian-based curriculum accredited for kindergarten all the way through twelfth grade. So my parents knew that once I got used to it, it would be something I could follow consistently until I graduated. It came with a series of CDs and videos, and the CDs connected me to a teacher, while the videos featured whatever book I was using. And my mom had a manual that outlined what the assignments were for a given day. There were a couple of marking periods where I had to take different tests for each subject, and there were quizzes and reports I had to do. Then we'd

pack up all my work in an envelope and send it to Flor-
ida, where it was reviewed, and a few weeks later I'd get
a report card. The best part was that the program was
designed to help you learn at your own pace, which was
helpful given my crazy schedule.

I'm a pretty good student who's always liked writing,
and as I've gotten older, I've also started to appreciate history more and more. I see it as a form of storytelling that
gets your imagination going. In one lesson, I remember
learning about the voyages of Christopher Columbus.
We have the technology to fly everywhere now, but back
then they had to sail on these rickety wooden boats.
There was no GPS, just maps, charts, and night-sky read-
ings that weren't very accurate—and somehow they still
made it. If you think about how Columbus and his crew
pushed themselves physically, mentally, and emotionally
to overcome all kinds of challenges and to survive the
dangers of the sea, it's mind-blowing.

As more of my teammates started homeschooling,
too, we would sit and do our work together, which made
it feel less isolating. We were all at different grade levels,
so we'd help each other if someone was struggling with
a subject we'd already covered. The older kids deserved
an A for taking care of the younger ones. Sometimes it
felt like we went to our own private school—albeit one
where everyone took advanced placement phys ed. What

we liked most about homeschooling was that it left so much more room in the day for practice. At that time, I was doing gymnastics roughly thirty-five hours a week. Later, as I began to compete more, my practice hours grew even longer. I was typically in the gym from eight thirty a.m. to one p.m. and from three thirty to five thirty p.m., six days a week. In between all that, I also managed to fit in meals, homework, and sleep. And over time I added physical therapy, special stretching sessions, and massages to my schedule. Some of you probably think massages are a luxury, but when you're an athlete who's constantly conditioning, they are legitimately necessary. Marta taught us that rehabilitation and taking care of our bodies is the *fifth* event: there's vault, bars, beam, floor, and then there's caring for ourselves. She considered self-care as important an event as all the others. It was something you couldn't skip—it's a very big part of the sport. I would add that it's also a very big part of life. It sounds funny, but sometimes you just need a relaxing massage or a mani-pedi. Other times you need to curl up with a good book and escape. When we drive ourselves as hard as we do—whether it's in our sports, our schoolwork, or our jobs—we can forget to take care of ourselves. Remembering to treat yourself well doesn't just apply to gymnastics. Everyone needs to take time out to rest and recharge. It really is okay to pamper yourself! It helps revive you and helps you do better when you return to the more challenging things you do every day. We should all tell our minds and bodies that we appreciate their role in making us achieve our goals. Between my intensive training schedule, my self-care regimen, and the kind of education I was getting through A Beka, I definitely got good at taking care of myself: mind, body, and spirit.

SWEATY PALMS, PRAYERS, AND PEPPERMINT OIL

CHAPTER 4

AT COMPETITIONS EVEN TO THIS DAY, BEFORE I
get on the equipment, I usually feel like I'm going to have
a heart attack. Those moments are still the worst for me,
and the jitters are my least favorite part of competing. I
don't know why my heart beats so fast—it's almost like
I can hear it—and my palms get all sweaty. But once I
start moving, I'm okay, especially on floor: as the music
begins playing, I feel extremely calm and comfortable;
by mid-routine, I realize how much fun I'm having; and
by the time I'm flipping or dancing, I've left all my worries behind. I can hear the crowd clapping to the music
and yet I can still focus at the same time. The difference

in how I feel before and during my floor routines never ceases to amaze me.

When I was younger, it was a bit different with the other events. Whenever I'd do beam routines, I'd be the most nervous, and it was written all over my face. I would be thinking, *Wow, I'm really scared—so scared that once I sit on the beam, I'll feel as if I can't stand up.* I remember my first Level 4 competition like it was yesterday. The meets always include events on the uneven bars, the balance beam, the vault, and floor exercise, and we refer to them simply as bars, beam, vault, and floor. At the Level 4 competition I was freaking out because I'd forgotten my beam routine and then I needed a spot on bars, which is when someone assists you in landing safely. But finally, I did floor and got a 9.5! I thought that part was the craziest thing.

There was another day I'll never forget. I was struggling hard with overcoming my nervousness, so my coach, Maggie, decided to shut off the music in the gym. There was nothing but dead silence. Then she made the whole class—kids, parents, and staff—sit on the floor and watch me do a beam routine. She made me do it over and over and over again until I felt comfortable. I hated it, but after that, the pressure of competing wasn't so bad.

Basically, I think it's the music that makes doing floor routines less stressful than doing bars or beam.

With floor, you have to multitask and dance to the beat at the same time. Because you're concentrating so much on that, there's no room for being nervous. That's probably why it's one of my favorite events. By contrast, when the music is off for bars and beam, it's just you, your thoughts, and the equipment. The skills you have to execute are so complex, it's easy for the thought of falling to creep into your head. Purposely turning off the music trained me to think only about the task at hand.

In addition to training hard, I do have two little tricks that help ease my nerves. A long time ago someone introduced me to peppermint oil. Whenever I'm feeling stressed before a competition, or whenever I get frustrated in practice, I'll take a minute or two away and just smell the oil. I feel like it clears my head. I started taking it to all my meets and telling everyone about it. When I joined *Dancing with the Stars*, the show bought me some, which I thought was kind of funny. I also have this little calming ritual I do once I'm on the beam, and it's practically involuntary at this point. I put my hand over my stomach, close my eyes, inhale, pause, and then exhale. As I feel my belly expand and contract with those breaths, the anxiety and adrenaline usually melt away. It's more than a habit now—it's almost like a part of my routine. A lot of people commented on it during the Olympics!

While peppermint oil and breathing techniques usually help ease my nerves and frustrations, unfortunately they don't do anything to help cure the occasional disappointment I feel after a bad meet. I have to rely on some of my mother's best advice for that. I remember this one awful competition after I'd moved up to the elite level. It was 2012 in St. Louis at the USA Gymnastics National Championships, which we all refer to as the P&G Championships, or the P&Gs for short. It was only the second big event I'd participated in in my life, and I came in twenty-first place that day. When the competition was all over, I started to cry. My coach seemed so disappointed in me, and of course, I was disappointed in myself. My mother came over and asked me what was wrong. When I told her, she said, "Do you know how many people in this world would love to be twenty-first at the P&Gs? Or how many people will never even get an opportunity to compete?" That was so like my mom; she firmly believes in the art of gratitude. Then she said, "Girl, we're not going to cry, we're going to celebrate!"

I couldn't believe it. *Celebrate?*

But she was right. Not many people ever get to where I was. So she wiped away my tears and bought me some ice cream. As we sat on the grass eating, I heard this little girl whisper to her dad, "Look, there's Laurie." When they got closer, the girl asked me for my autograph, and we took a picture together. It was adorable to see how happy she was. Whoever those people were, they saw something in me, and in that moment, they helped restore some of my confidence. Now whenever I'm fangirling around people I admire, I think about that moment—you never know how much your appreciation can lift up someone else's spirits.

Later that afternoon my mom and I talked some more, and she reminded me that a lot of times disappointment is what helps you grow. It presents an opportunity to improve. She told me that if I'd done the best that I could in that moment, under those particular circumstances, then I was only responsible for my own reaction, because that's the only thing I was really in control of. I cannot be responsible for the reactions of fans, teammates, judges, coaches, or anyone else—which is an important lesson all athletes need to learn at some point. You can tell that my mom is a wise and spiritual woman. There's a lot of prayer and faith happening in my family. More than anything—even more than peppermint oil—that's what keeps me calm and centered. I find it makes it much easier to deal with the kinds of mental and physical stresses I face.

I have to admit that as rough as those first

competitions were, they ended up being pretty positive experiences. Now I recover from disappointments more quickly and with more optimism, and when I find I'm nervous, I tell myself not to worry, because I'm right where I'm supposed to be. There's no reason to be anxious. All I have to do is just chill and go with it.

GO TIME!

CHAPTER 5

DURING THE STRETCH FROM 2009 TO 2012, I WAS working my way up the USA Gymnastics ranks to Level 10. Every so often, I'd look back and think, *Oh, I've come so far, I can't even believe I'm at this point right now.* Then in 2012, after having passed Level 10, I was able to begin competing regularly at the junior elite level. I was twelve years old at the time (you can't be a senior elite until the year you turn sixteen). All I can say is: when you finally step into those higher-level competitions and you see girls in your age group doing all these amazing skills, the reality hits you. You have a moment where you just take it all in and think, *Wow,* I'm *a part of that.*

Now, before I tell you about all the competitions I started doing, let me explain how scoring works. To win an individual title on an apparatus in a competition, you have to have the best score of the meet on that apparatus (for example, to win the title for beam, you must place first on beam in the overall competition). To win the all-around, you have to have the best overall combined score of each apparatus event—the vault, bars, beam, and floor events—during that competition.

Gymnastics scores are generally calculated on two basic components: how difficult the routine is and how well the routine is executed. To score for *difficulty*, the judges begin at zero and add points for how well you meet each of the required skills, how well you performed the most difficult skills in your routine, and how well you connected two of the tougher techniques together to form what we call a "combination." To score for *execution*—basically, how well you did overall—the judges start at ten and subtract points for mistakes, such as faltering on a landing, not keeping your toes pointed, or separating your legs when they should be together. Each of the eight most difficult skills in your routine have assigned values according to the sport's Code of Points, but the judges can award extra points when very difficult skills are combined well. The more fluid the connections between difficult skills, the higher the score you get—that is, unless you make a mistake. (For this reason, sometimes being too ambitious can cost you points!) To arrive at your final score, the difficulty and execution scores are added up, and then "neutral points"—points deducted for things like stepping out of bounds or taking too long to complete your routine—are subtracted. You'll notice that there is no such thing as a perfect 10 anymore, because if you add enough difficulty to your routine, you can earn way more than ten points. In fact, at the Olympic level, it's not unusual to see scores ranging between 13 and 16.

With that taken care of, let's move on to the action!

My first Level 10 event was the Secret US Classic—which we refer to as the Secret Classic. I remember I wore a hot-pink leotard that day (I love that color!), and the lights were really bright, and being on a podium frightened me a little. When you have a large crowd like that, the equipment is put on a raised platform roughly three feet off the ground so the audience can see better. I had never been at a competition big enough to require a podium, but there were a lot of people at this meet. The whole thing was a little intimidating until I got used to it and just focused on my routines.

I actually fell on bars that day, which scared me at first. But in order to move on from there, I had to pretend that nothing had happened. I took a deep breath and told myself, *You know what, we still have the rest of the competition. This is your first time here. Just give it your all.* And I did.

Although that fall on bars got me off to a rough start, it all came down to vault. I needed a 13.45 in order to qualify for the P&Gs in St. Louis, and that's the exact score I got! It was insane. And I also ended up placing eleventh all-around in the junior division.

It was around this time that I made another big leap: I was asked to train at the USA Gymnastics National Team Training Camp. As you might remember, this camp is also located at Karolyi Ranch in Texas, just like the developmental camp I'd been going to for years. Although it was the same exact place, the National Team practices were held at different times with a different group of girls, and the vibe was totally different, too (i.e., much more serious). The developmental camp works with up-and-coming junior elites, while the National Team Training Camp is where all the highest-level gymnasts go to train—essentially, the girls working toward international competitions and the Olympics.

As soon as I arrived at the National Team camp, I was surrounded by the best of the best. It was very intimidating. I asked myself, *Am I supposed to be here?* I watched the other girls both inside and outside the gym. I observed the way they were doing a certain skill, how they put on their grips, what they did to keep their hands from hurting or ripping on bars. And since we roomed together, I got to know them all well, too. I saw how they managed their time and how they relaxed. And it was cool because we all became friends.

GETTING OUT OF THE COUNTRY

CHAPTER 6

MY FIRST MEET OF 2013 WAS THE WORLD OLYMPIC
Gymnastics Academy Classic, known as the WOGA Classic. I placed second in the all-around and felt great. I'd done super well on every single one of my events across the board!

Later, in July of that same year, I competed in the American Classic in Huntsville, Texas, where I placed first on floor, second in the all-around, and third on both beam and vault. It turned out that Jordyn Wieber, one of the gymnasts who went to the 2012 Olympics, was also staying in my hotel. When I saw her walking around one night, I snuck out and got a picture with her—she was someone I'd really looked up to, which made it even cooler.

After my thirteenth birthday, I was added to the USA Gymnastics Junior National Team. The National Team is usually chosen in June, sometimes in August, and you get to stay on the team for a year. It's made up of eleven or twelve American girls who have qualified because of their high scores at competitions, and it's only the National Team members who get to compete internationally. I felt such a sense of accomplishment having been chosen, and the whole rest of the summer was so exciting! I went to Chicago for the Secret Classic again, and this time I placed sixth all-around and won the floor exercise title. But what was most memorable for me was returning to the P&G Championships in St. Louis, where I felt I'd done so poorly the year before. By this point, with enough competitions under my belt, neither the bright lights, nor the crowds, nor being on a podium could bother me. It was a two-day competition, and I remember hitting all my events. ("Hitting," by the way, means that I killed it, doing all the skills in my routine super well.) I placed second on bars and floor and tied for third on beam with the very talented Alexis Vasquez. But the real highlight was winning the silver medal in the junior all-around competition, with a total score of 116.650. I came in behind Bailie Key, who is not only one of the best junior gymnasts in the world, but also one of the people I admire most in the sport. She was an awesome teammate and someone I was hoping to emulate, so it amazed me when I scored almost as well as her that day. It took me a minute to process what an accomplishment that was!

As I went to more and more of these events, I started noticing a funny pattern: if I had a horrible warm-up, I usually ended up hitting a really nice routine. It doesn't work that way for everyone. Sometimes a bad warm-up can throw people off. But I tend to think warm-ups are where I work out my jitters. Now, I'm literally known for my bad warm-ups! Luckily, bad warm-ups were translating to amazing meets, and with all this great momentum behind me, I felt happy about my national competitions and was looking forward to my next big step.

When I first began competing on the national level, people would constantly say, "All you have to do is get out of the country." If anyone overheard us, they'd have thought we were fugitives! But what they meant is that you have to be good enough for Marta and her staff at the USA National Team to trust that you'll hit your routines when they send you to compete internationally. Once you're "out of the country," you're competing on a global level. It means you're one of the best in the world.

By September 2013, Marta and the other coaches

did trust me enough, and they sent me to the Japan Junior International in Yokohama. I was so excited I could hardly wait. Unfortunately, my family couldn't make the trip with me, but they watched every second of the competition on Livestream. Marta wasn't at that competition, either—it was just Bailie and me there competing for the United States, plus my coach, Maggie, and Bailie's coach, too. Bailie was the perfect person to go with, because she'd been to a couple of international meets already. She knew what she was doing, so I just kind of followed her lead to avoid doing anything wrong.

One of the biggest challenges when you're competing internationally is getting used to the time difference. I could always make the adjustment when I flew from New Jersey to Texas for camp, since that's only a one-hour change. But the time difference between New Jersey and Japan is fourteen hours! That meant that while we were competing at four o'clock in the afternoon in Japan, it was really six o'clock in the morning at home.

To help us manage the time change, we slept on the flight there and scheduled a workout for the evening we arrived. But I still had a hard time sleeping at the hotel. I just wasn't used to the beds: they were very hard because there was a wooden plank under the mattress, and the pillow was like a giant beanbag. Apparently, those types of beds and pillows help improve your posture, but they didn't do much for my sleep.

Since I was tossing and turning in the middle of the night anyway, I'd get up and call my family and talk to them just as they were getting home from work and school. I learned that Bailie had the same idea: the walls were so thin between our separate rooms that when she was FaceTiming with her parents, I could hear their conversations, and whenever I was Skyping with mine, she could hear us. To make sure we were awake in the morning when we were supposed to be, we would bang on the wall and check that the other one was out of bed. We didn't want to oversleep and miss practice or the competition!

In the end, the Japan Junior International was kind of a rough meet. I was not only tired, but since it was my first international competition, I was nervous, too. I fell on bars, did great on my individual beam final qualifying score, and then fell on beam in the final. In the end I scored a 56.750 in the all-around to win a bronze medal, and I took third on vault, fourth on floor exercise, and sixth on beam.

Around Thanksgiving that same year I went to the International Junior Mexican Cup in Acapulco. While I was excited to travel again, I don't think people realize just how difficult it is to be away from your family on holidays or to miss family vacations. But I have no regrets, because I was doing what I loved. And besides, our host country on that trip was so thoughtful, and they held a special Thanksgiving dinner for us. The food was great, and it would have been nice to spend more time with our new friends—but we have strict rules before competitions, and getting back to the hotel early to get a good night's sleep is one of them.

The International Junior Mexican Cup was a big competition for me. Marta was there and so were some senior team members I'd watched and admired for such a long time. I recall doing my beam routine over and over during pre-competition practice and hitting it every single time. That was a great feeling—but what was even better was that Marta noticed. I couldn't believe my ears when she told me my beam routine was absolutely beautiful. It's a well-known fact that Marta doesn't give compliments easily!

At the competition, vault went well. After that it was kind of back and forth for me and Bailie: I made floor and she fell. Then she made bars and I fell. So just before beam, I got really scared and started to have a mini meltdown—*What if I fall in that event, too?* In a competition like that one, you're always thinking about what every little move means for the team. But the rest of the team encouraged me, saying, "Hey, you're fine.

Stop stressing out. You got it!" So I went up there, and of course, I got my cool back and beam went well. The team, which was composed of me, Bailie Key, Veronica Hults, and Emily Gaskins, won a gold medal that day, and I took second place behind Bailie in the all-around.

As it turned out, Marta looked closely at our individual scores even during team competitions. We were all on Marta's radar, but she had so many girls in the program, it's not like she saw me in action all the time, since the seniors tend to be her priority. When she was choosing who to bring to Acapulco, I suspect she'd seen I'd come in second at the P&Gs. Even with that, I have to believe that seeing how close I came to the hottest competitor at the Mexican Cup was mind-blowing for her and the others. I mean, it was pretty mind-blowing for me! I was only three-tenths of a point behind Bailie. I usually don't pay attention to other people's scores during competitions, because I have to keep my head on my own performance. So seeing the end results was pretty wild.

If all that wasn't crazy enough, the night after the competition we were having dinner by the beach and I looked over to see Nadia Comaneci sitting with some of the other coaches at a table near us. (If you don't know who Nadia is, your parents will! Everyone in their generation knows her, because at the 1976 Summer Olympics in Montreal, when she was just fourteen, she became the first gymnast in Olympic history to be awarded the perfect score of 10.0. In the days that followed, she also received six more perfect 10s, taking home three gold medals. It was amazing! Then, four years later, during the 1980 Olympics in Moscow, she added two more gold medals to her collection.) Nadia, who's from Romania, is one of my all-time favorite heroes, and now she was sitting a few feet away from me. I was shaking a little when I saw her, but I still went over to introduce myself. I said, "Hi, I'm Laurie," and gave her a big hug. She was so nice. She smiled and said, "I know who you are. I watched you at the competition. Keep going. You're going to be great." I nearly passed out. All I kept thinking was, *Nadia Comaneci knows who I am!* I held on to her words for a few minutes, and after that, I think I just floated away.

Nadia was trained by Bela Karolyi at the experimental gymnastics camp that he and Marta established in Romania before they came to the United States. While it was Nadia who first inspired the world to fall in love with artistic gymnastics, it's been Bela and Marta who've kept that love alive by fostering the careers of so many amazing gymnasts since then—gymnasts ranging from Mary Lou Retton to Simone Biles! This sport owes so much to all three of them. *I* owe so much to all three of them.

MY BIG BREAK

CHAPTER 7

I HAD STARTED OFF 2013 BELIEVING THAT THINGS were just going to get better and better. I'm an optimist by nature, and my experiences in international competitions during the previous season had given me added confidence that with continued practice, I'd have the skills and opportunities to go even further. But early that winter, something unexpected happened: I was practicing a skill on beam—it was a handspring also known as a triple series—and on the third mount step-out, I slipped and landed on my wrist. After X-rays, I was told I had a distal radius fracture. The radius is the larger of the two bones in your forearm, and the lower end of that bone—the part closest to your wrist—is called the distal. That's the part I injured.

I had actually fractured my wrist once before. That time, I had been stumbling a lot in practice, and I eventually realized my wrist had been hurting the whole day. I told my mom and she took to me to get it checked right away. It turned out my wrist was fractured. Nothing in particular had happened to cause it—I think the damage was just caused by overuse.

The timing of the distal radius fracture, though, was extremely frustrating. It meant I'd have to sit out some competitions I'd been looking forward to. It was crushing to get that kind of news, but you know in the back of your mind that the best athletes in the world train themselves to deal mentally with injury the same way they train physically. I also knew that it was far from being a career-ending injury, and I was confident that I would bounce back before the next meet season. I let myself sulk for a day or two, and then I decided to make the best of it. I kind of knew the drill: I would have to rest it and let it heal, but that didn't mean practice, and everything else in my life, had to stop.

A big part of recovery is doing what the doctor tells you. Listening to my physician, Dr. David R. Gentile, was easy because he explained everything so well. He specializes in the treatment of sports-related trauma, particularly elbow, hand, shoulder, and wrist injuries. Luckily, when you're young, fractures tend to mend faster. Because you're still growing, your body is already doing the necessary work to build and strengthen your bones. Even so, being in a cast for nearly eight weeks felt like an eternity. But another part of recovery is being patient. For the first few weeks, the cast came up past my elbow. Then Dr. Gentile cut it down to just above my wrist, so I felt a lot less restricted.

The entire time I was in a cast, I made sure I stayed in great shape. I continued to do whatever skills and conditioning I could. I didn't do anything that involved my hands, of course, but I did work my legs a lot, and as a result they became so much stronger. I thought, *Well, I can still do a no-handed cartwheel*—so I did! I ran every exercise possible to keep the rest of my body in peak condition while my wrist healed.

When you're an athlete who's sustained an injury, a lot goes into keeping your body healthy. The parts you use repeatedly are often vulnerable to reinjury. Even after I healed, I continued to see Dr. Gentile, and I learned so much from him. He promoted self-care before, during, and after practice and competition. As I mentioned, my mother and sister are both social workers, so they taught me that self-care is not just physical. It's mental and emotional, too. Each time I got injured, they told me that everything happens for a reason, so I should just embrace it and think about what that reason might be—maybe this was simply my body's way of saying it needed time off. And at moments like that, you must practice patience, stay positive, and even be resourceful about continuing your training. When I look back, I see that my whole approach to workouts during that period helped improve all those qualities in me. While some people would call my wrist fracture a tough break, it might just have been my lucky break, because it helped me prepare for the tough challenges still ahead.

After finally rebounding from the fracture and thinking the worst was over, I sustained yet another injury. And sadly, it would turn out to be much worse than the one to my wrist. . . .

I was training in Texas at the time. I remember the day it happened so clearly: it was early June 2014, about six months after the fracture, and I was doing a vault, and as I landed, I twisted my knee and fell to the ground. I heard something pop, and when I stood up, my leg just slipped out from under me. My knee didn't hurt right away, although it felt uncomfortable to walk. I told the trainers what I was experiencing, but there were no visible signs that anything was wrong. Eventually Marta came over and looked at it and told me not to practice for the rest of the day. I took her advice, and by the end of the week, my knee was super swollen and the pain had kicked in, and I still needed to stay off it. We had it checked out and when I returned home, we got the news that I had a dislocated knee, a torn patella ligament, and a bruised MCL—all from one fall!

The patella ligament, just so you know, is what secures the top of the knee to the bone underneath it. When I tore mine, my kneecap slipped out of place. The MCL is one of four ligaments vital to the function and support of the knee; it runs along the inside of the knee, where it connects the thighbone and shinbone. The whole area was so swollen it looked like I had a water balloon under my skin! When we realized I was going to need surgery, I actually don't remember the emotions I was feeling. As soon as we were told what the damage was, I knew there was nothing I could do about it. It was almost awkward that it happened when it did, right when I finally had most of my skills back after my wrist injury.

My mom was the one who stepped in and said, okay, we need to rest it and repair it as soon as possible so you heal and come back quickly. We knew what we had to do, and we set out to do it. We got in touch with USA Gymnastics immediately to get the name of a doctor who had experience treating this type of serious injury. They recommended Dr. John Fulkerson, an orthopedic surgeon who specializes in sports medicine. He was ranked among the top 1 percent of orthopedic surgeons in the country, and they told us he was the "it man" in the field for this specific set of challenges—and once we drove up to his offices in Connecticut and met with him, we agreed.

After examining my knee, Dr. Fulkerson looked at me very calmly and promised that he was going to get me back to good health. I was so grateful to be seeing someone who had performed thousands of procedures on injuries like mine, many on athletes who'd returned to their competitive sports afterward. I had been frightened before then, trying not to think the worst. The fact that Dr. Fulkerson was so confident made me a little more confident. It gave me hope.

Dr. Fulkerson's positivity and understanding meant a lot not only to me, it meant a lot to my family, too. My parents had never pushed me into the world of gymnastics. This wasn't their dream—it was mine. Their dream was that I be as happy as I could be, and because I loved gymnastics, they let me follow my bliss. There were definitely times when they looked at each other and asked, "Are we doing the right thing? Is this really good for our daughter?" I'm not sure they always knew the answer. But whenever they asked me, my response was "Yes." It was never a big, long, drawn-out conversation. My dad would just look at me and say, "Are we good?" That one little question packed a lot of meaning. Whatever my answer was going to be, you could be sure he and my mom would be on board with it.

After we formulated a plan of attack with Dr. Fulker-son, I must admit that I was still scared. But I knew in my bones—even the broken and dislocated ones—that this was what I wanted to do, that this was what I needed to do to get back out there one day. So when I said, "We're good," my parents supported me in every way and we all moved ahead together.

ABRA-CADAVER!

CHAPTER 8

AS YOU KNOW BY NOW, MY DOCTOR KEPT HIS
promise: the surgery went well, and in time, I did get full
use of my knee back. But my recovery wasn't easy.

Right after the surgery at the end of June, I remember
lying totally still on the couch, and I wasn't even moving
my leg, yet it felt so awful. I thought, *If it hurts right now,*
what is it going to feel like when I'm tumbling? I couldn't
imagine it. Even when I slept, I was in pain. Gymnasts'
legs can sometimes twitch at night. Right after the surgery, my leg was so stiff that when the twitching started,
it would wake me up. It hurt more than you can know.

Aside from the physical pain, I was sad because I was

no longer sure I'd ever be able to return to gymnastics. My mother didn't have to say anything, but I could see the worry on her face, too. I had to prove not only to the people around me that I could come back, but I had to prove it to myself, too. I let myself wallow in those sad feelings for a few days, and then I came up with a plan. I decided that I would just take my time, that I'd follow the therapy process as perfectly as possible and I wouldn't rush anything, so that when I did come back, I would come back stronger than ever.

The very next day, I returned to doing my usual stretches up against the wall in my room. When my mother saw me doing that, she was confused. Actually, she was confused *and* concerned. I said, "Look, Mom, you don't understand. This is not over. This is what I want." At the time, I don't think I could've explained why I felt that way, but when I reflect on it now, I'm sure I wanted to get back to gymnastics because I am happiest and most comfortable when my body is in motion. I am pretty sassy and have a lot to say, and I love to talk more than anyone I know, and I love to write as well. But my body has a lot to say, too. It says the things I can't say with words. That's why I love floor so much: I am free to let my emotions flow in those routines; it's when my body is at its most expressive.

Even though I didn't explain my feelings exactly like

that at the time, my mother heard me. A little later that day she took a picture of me doing those stretches—I still have it on my phone (I've shared it in this book). I keep it to remind me of the determination I had in such a difficult moment.

The same way I'd worked my legs when I couldn't use my hands, I worked my arms when I couldn't use my legs. I was not giving up. When I wasn't training, I was watching gymnastics videos or following how my friends were doing at their meets. That year my Monmouth Gymnastics (MG) Elite teammate Jazmyn Foberg, whom we all call Jazzy, took the number one spot at Nationals. I remember being glued to the TV as she competed at the P&Gs in Pittsburgh. It was such a great moment for her. I was tweeting about it, cheering her on, and generally making sure she felt my support. But at the same time, I wanted to recover and get back out there myself. I missed it. It seemed as if all the same lessons I'd learned when I fractured my wrist were being reinforced: I knew I had to be patient, positive, motivated, and resourceful. I always finish what I start, and this time was no exception. I wasn't about to quit.

What I learned about fully recovering from an injury is that it's something only you can decide to do for yourself. It helps to have a strong community, but until you know you're ready to push for it, there's nothing anyone else can say to convince you. For a long time, I didn't talk to anyone about what I was feeling. I would just put my head down and do the work. Lots of times I was fighting against myself.

Everyone would tell me that I could do it and that I was strong, but I think the person who understood what I was going through the most was my brother. Marcus just sat with me when I was tired and told me he understood how hard it was. That was all he said, and I appreciated it. I know he'd been around some resilient athletes in his track days. He saw that even the tough Division I athletes he knew had fragile moments after a big injury. He understood that I was competing at an even higher level, so there was even more at stake.

It also helped to talk to my physical therapist, Malvin Torralba. I told him how nervous I was, and he said, "Then don't go back before I release you. You know I'm not going to release you until I know you're really strong enough to get out there again, right?" And he was right. When I did finally return in November, I was still scared to do things I thought might hurt. Everyone I worked with at the gym and at the ranch reassured me that they wouldn't let me do anything I couldn't do, though. They pushed me hard, and even though there were times I thought it was too hard, they remained true to their word and never pushed me beyond my abilities. One reason I got through those tough workouts was Dr. Jidong Sun. She got her medical training in Beijing, so she knew all the best rehab practices used on elite gymnasts in China and applied them to my recovery. And Dr. Sunny Shen gave me acupuncture, which helps your body heal itself. When you have regular acupuncture treatments, you're making sure the wear and tear of daily practice is being addressed before small problems turn into big ones.

There are so many other examples of the kind of support I received from people during that difficult recovery time: friends, family, doctors, coaches, teammates—everyone rallied around me. And possibly the most incredible act of kindness came from someone who never knew me and whom I will never have the chance to thank. One of the amazing things about my surgery is that Dr. Fulkerson restored my torn ligament by using a piece of a cadaver! The donated tissue was grafted to my damaged tissue to help mend and strengthen it. By the magic of medical science and the generosity of tissue donors like mine, many athletes and people who've had serious or multiple injuries to their ligaments have been able to make a comeback in their sport or life. I know I'm very grateful to my donor and his family, and I'm sure others who have had the same procedure are grateful to theirs, too.

I definitely had my fair share of struggles throughout 2014, but by the time it was over, I was a much stronger person mentally, physically, and emotionally—and everyone around me could sense it. I was finally ready for a new chapter in my gymnastics career to begin. Though as mature as that sounds, I still approached my sport with all the pent-up, hyperactive energy of a fourteen-year-old. While I had to adopt a serious mind-set for much of that year, I was still a kid, and I didn't want to give up that part of me yet—if I was going to continue on this path, I still wanted it to be fun.

BRING IT ON!

CHAPTER 9

SPEAKING OF FUN, THERE ARE FEW PLACES IN THE world more fun and exciting than Italy! I'd always wanted to go there, and in March 2015, that dream came true when I competed for the City of Jesolo Trophy.

Whenever the USA Gymnastics team competes internationally, we usually arrive a few days early so we can adjust to the time difference, to what we're eating, and to the equipment we're using. My teammates Jazzy and Norah Flatley—two of my favorite people in the world—were on this trip, too. I feel like I've known them both forever, and in some ways, with Norah, I really have. Norah and I first met at TOPs camp, when we were much younger and were being tested to see what our potential was. We didn't see each other for several years after that, but when I became a junior, I saw her at the ranch and thought, *Hey, wait, don't I know her from somewhere?* We were happy to reconnect because we'd had so much fun together before. When we'd bunked together at camp, we'd make shadow puppets on the wall at night and tell stories. It was great to have extra time with Norah and Jazzy in a place as special and vibrant as Italy. We fell completely in love with the food, the architecture, the gondolas, and the people. But the craziest thing happened before we even got there. . . .

I was at camp in Texas, and Marta was deciding who to take to the upcoming international competition this time around. I had to qualify on both bars and beam in order to go. As it happened, a rip had reopened on my wrist (a rip is when a flap of skin, sometimes several layers thick, comes off on the palm or wrist due to friction between the hands and the parallel or uneven bars). And the rip seemed to be infected. I wanted to compete outside the country again, and I also knew that Jesolo was just a little bit north of Venice, a city I'd always wanted to see. I couldn't let this opportunity pass me by, so on the day of the first trial I said to myself, *I'll try to qualify, and if it doesn't work out, then it doesn't work out. It wasn't meant to be.* That's kind of my philosophy when I'm not sure which way things are going to go for me. I've always had confidence that if I'm supposed to succeed, I will, and if I don't, God will just redirect me toward the path I should be on. Marcus reminded me of that a lot after I had my surgery, and he was right. With that mind-set firmly in place, I put on my grips and did my routine. A few hours later, when my wrist looked worse than before, I was worried. Trials were continuing into the next day, and that's when I would have to qualify for beam. I knew the infection wouldn't be clear by then if I didn't get it checked out, so I asked to be taken to the hospital and they gave me antibiotics to clear it up. When I finally got back to my room late that night, I was stressing because I really wanted to go to Italy. I called my mom and she said, "Laurie, you don't have to do this. You don't have to go to Jesolo. I'll come to Texas and pick you up." After everything that had happened the year before, she and my father didn't want me doing anything that would jeopardize my health. But I was still determined to try, because the lesson I'd learned from all my injuries was that you can never take anything for granted. If you don't try to work your way back, the opportunity is over; if you try your hardest to come back and it doesn't happen for you, then you can at least say you gave it your best effort.

Early the next morning I pushed through, and I'm happy I did because I qualified for beam. Still, it wasn't certain that I was going: Marta was very clear with me that if I wasn't healed by the time we had to leave, they couldn't take me. I had to make sure I got better before I got on that plane . . . and I did.

In the end, I guess it was meant to be, because the competition went well for me. As my mom likes to say: I rocked the house! I ended up being crowned junior all-around champion with a score of 57.650. In the junior event finals, I earned additional gold medals on bars and floor with scores of 14.400 and 14.500 respectively. I was happier than a singing gondolier!

Winning the Jesolo Trophy was a victory for me on many levels. I went into it wanting to show the people who were putting their faith in me that my past injuries weren't going to hold me back—and that, if anything, they had made me better. That's exactly the message I think I conveyed.

Italy positively influenced the next few competitions for me, too. In the lead-up to 2016—an Olympic year—our meet season was different. We weren't competing constantly, because our coaches didn't want us to overexert ourselves. Our biggest competitions in 2015 were mostly held in the summer, so during the winter and spring we worked on skills and basics or on new skills we wanted to add to our routines to upgrade them. But because the competition in Italy happened so early in the year, we just kept doing routines from that point onward. As a result, my routines got more and more consistent.

By the time June came around, I went into the national competitions thinking, *All right, this is mine. I got this.* That's probably when I first started saying that now-famous expression to myself. During practice for most competitions, my teammates and I usually warmed up by doing pressure sets, where everyone watches while you perform your routine. I could always hear them cheering for me in the background, saying things like, "Come on, Laurie, you can do it. You got this." Eventually, as the Olympics drew closer, I noticed that I was practicing more and more by myself. Because I had a lot of doctor appointments, my schedule changed and there were a lot of times it was just me and my coach in the gym alone for workouts. That's when I began talking to myself, kind of mimicking what my teammates used to say when they cheered me on. I found that saying what they would say, especially "You got this," helped to calm and focus me.

Sure enough, after assuring myself that the next meet was mine, I hit all my routines at the Secret Classic and ended up winning the junior all-around with a score of 58.450. I also won vault with a 14.900 and bars with a 15.00 score. I placed third on beam with a 14.200 and tied with Deanne Soza for floor, scoring a 14.350. It was one of my favorite competitions until that point. I could just feel that this was going to be my breakthrough year.

Then I hit all my routines at the P&Gs in Indianapolis: by the end of the two-day competition, I had won the junior all-around, the title on bars with a combined two-day score of 30.100, silver on floor, and bronze on beam and vault. Though it didn't exactly start out too well. . . .

On the first day we were leading off with vault. During practice I kept getting lost in my twist and landing on my back. (I told you I was known for my bad warm-ups!) That really frightened me. I didn't know what to do. Just minutes before I competed, my coach said, "Don't worry about it. Just go for it." So I took a leap of faith, and by some miracle, I was able to finish the twist. After it was all over, she said, "You can't give me a heart attack like that. Next time, don't do that. It scared me." It was such a crazy way to start off the meet, but it made me realize that I'm not the only one who stresses out at competitions. Coaches have to make some tough judgment calls that weigh on them, too. Thankfully, the rest of the meet was great.

My teammate Jazzy was in the lead on the first day, and my score was 57.950. I tried not to think too much about that and focused instead on enjoying the competition and everything around me. I followed up with a score of 59.550 on the second day. We ended with the floor exercise, and after Jazzy and I each did our routines, I thought we had tied. There's this video of us jumping up and down when my score came up because we thought we were both going to come in first. But in reality, I was one-tenth of a point above her. It was *so* close.

As you can imagine, one of the tough things about competing is that a lot of times you like and respect the other gymnasts. That's how I feel about Jazzy. She's such an amazing person. She's so focused that no matter what the task is, she will not stop pushing until she gets the job done. She's a real go-getter. As for me, I do freak out at times (but I do the best I can in the moment and then I let it go). In that way, we balance each other out. But even when you're really close with someone like that, you can't feel bad about placing ahead of them or behind them in any competition. So at the P&Gs, I thought, *Thank goodness my hard work finally paid off! All the repetitions I did came together at the last minute and I was able to hit those routines.* At the same time, I was reminding Jazzy of how good a job she did, too! And if I'd come in second, I'd have thought, *Okay, there's always a next time.* In situations like that, when I come in behind a teammate, I always try to congratulate her. I think it's important to acknowledge that she worked hard and deserves her success. (Not to get too far ahead, but I did that at the

Olympics with Sanne Wevers of the Netherlands, the girl who won gold for beam. I saw her crying because she was so excited, so I walked over and said, "I watched you in practice. You are such a hard worker. You definitely deserve this. Congratulations." I didn't think, *Ah man, I should have gotten that first-place medal.* Instead I thought, *Wow, I'm proud of you, but I'm proud of me, too, for getting that second place.*) I guess I can do that because I know how much any gymnast puts into getting to our level of skill. It deserves our mutual respect.

The next big event after the P&Gs brought me back to Japan, where I'd had my very first international competition in 2013. I was a lot more comfortable than I'd been that first time. Jazzy was in the competition with me, too, and we both had so much fun. It's one of those experiences I'm never going to forget. We got to tour Tokyo and visit these beautiful Japanese temples. I made a lot of Japanese friends, and we all ended up trading team pins. It was such a great experience. The culture was completely new to us, and as I mentioned about our trip to Italy, even the gymnastic equipment in Japan was different. The texture of the material didn't feel like what we were used to in the United States. One thing I remember clearly is that the vault runway didn't have a platform under it, so it was much harder than ours. But we all adjusted quickly.

I ended up winning the all-around there, too, as well as floor and vault. I also earned silver medals on beam and bars. I was happy that it was such a consistent and steady meet. It was definitely my best career performance up to that moment. But even though people started saying I was unstoppable, I knew I still had to grow. I was determined to double down and work even harder to meet my goals. It was always flattering to hear people say, "You're coming up so quickly, you're amazing," but I did have to just say "Thank you" and then ignore the compliment. I couldn't let those words sit in my head like that, just in case my mind got the message that it could stop pushing so hard. I had to tell myself, *You still have work to do; it's not over yet.*

A FAR CRY
FROM OVER

CHAPTER 10

I KNOW THIS IS A WEIRD QUESTION, BUT HAVE YOU ever had a premonition? You know, where you're positive something is about to happen to you? You can close your eyes and see a future event unfold before you as clearly as if it were a memory?

Well, I woke up on New Year's Day in 2016 having that exact experience. I'm not kidding. I'd always known that gymnastics was something I was supposed to be doing. From a very early age, I'd had this feeling that my career was already planned out for me and that I was simply putting things into motion the day I pointed to Shawn Johnson on TV and said, "I want to do that, too!" I almost can't imagine that one event *not* happening—my whole life would be entirely different. But it did happen, and nearly eleven years later I was getting out of bed on January 1, 2016, knowing not only that gymnastics was what I was supposed to be doing but also knowing beyond a shadow of a doubt that 2016 was my year.

I came out of my bedroom and sat down at the table with my family and said, "Guys, it's time." I'm not sure they knew what I meant, so I continued, "Watch where I'm going to be in July. I promise you, I'm going to show the world why I love artistic gymnastics so much." They all looked at me with big smiles and my mom said, "We know, baby."

Each of my family members will tell you that they've always sensed I was destined for something special. I'm all about embracing life in a big way, and whether I was going to be a gymnast, a dancer, or an actress, they knew I loved putting myself out there and entertaining others. Even the way I tumbled on my brother's bed after school, showing him moves I'd just made up, and the way my little toddler body mimicked my siblings' kicks in their karate class, suggested I was going to be an athlete or a performer or both. When my family and I went on a cruise to the western Caribbean, I was thrilled because they had a karaoke night. I was only five years old and

I bounded onto the stage and started singing a Mariah Carey song. I didn't know all the lyrics, so my sister joined me and started to sing along, too. But I pushed her aside and was like, "No, no, no. Go away. I got it!" I've learned how to share the limelight better since then, but the point of this story is that I don't get embarrassed easily. Whenever I falter, I pick myself up and try again.

While my whole family was sure I'd succeed at something big one day, it was Marcus who predicted I'd go to the Olympics. He first called it when he was in seventh grade, and later, his Facebook, Instagram, and Twitter accounts would also prove he'd accurately predicted it. He was telling the world about me through social media as early as his freshman year in high school—that was seven years ago! In fact, on Marcus's high school prom night, the two of us took a photo together that he posted online. The caption read *Before prom with a future Olympian*. After I made the Olympic team, some of his friends remembered that picture and found it. He claims it's undeniable evidence that he knew all along I'd make it.

I kicked off 2016 by making my debut as a senior on the US team. When I returned to Italy to compete in the annual City of Jesolo competition in March, I was going as one of the "big girls." My faith in myself was at an all-time high, and I was so excited because I'd wanted to be a senior for so long.

The morning of the competition, I had such a great start. I was rooming with my teammate Emily Gaskins, who is a pure joy to be around. When I woke up, the room was dark, but in a matter of seconds Emily was jumping up and down all over the place, raising the shades, shouting, "Meet Day, Meet Day! Get up, it's Meet Day!" To her it didn't matter that we would be competing against each other; she just wanted us to enjoy life, the event ahead of us, and the fact that we were there together. Everything about her energy was screaming, *Isn't this the best day in the world???* I love having team spirit and being encouraged by others, and in my mind, Emily is great at both. That morning she filled my cup with her energy to the point of overflowing, which is one of the reasons I think I did so well.

In Jesolo I earned a bronze medal in the all-around with a score of 58.550, coming in behind two other seniors, Ragan Smith and Gabby Douglas. Ragan is such a gifted gymnast, and Gabby, of course, had been the 2012 Olympic all-around champion. I also earned a silver medal on vault and a gold medal on balance beam ahead of Ragan and Aly Raisman, who was also a 2012 Olympian.

The second international competition of the year was in April. It was the Pacific Rim Gymnastics Championships (known as Pac Rim) in Everett, Washington. I didn't have much experience as a senior, so Marta put me on that team to gain more. The team consisted of myself, Aly Raisman, Ragan Smith, Simone Biles (the three-time world all-around champion), Ashton Locklear, and Brenna Dowell. Because I was surrounded by so much talent, I just remember thinking, *Watch and learn.*

My goal was to hit as many of my routines as possible, and not only did I do that, the entire team hit their routines, too! Everyone was so proud of us. It was such a great feeling. I had an all-around score of 59.800, which contributed to the team's first-place finish, and I also placed third individually, behind Simone and Aly. I didn't earn the all-round bronze, though, because of a rule limiting medals to two gymnasts per country (in case one country was dominating and might sweep all the others). The bronze went to Nagi Kajita of Japan instead. But it was great knowing that I came in right after two of my strongest teammates. I also qualified for the beam finals, but it was decided that neither Simone nor I would compete in the event finals because the team management wanted us as rested as we could be for the Olympic Trials. That turned out to be a very good plan, because not everything in 2016 went as smoothly as it first appeared it would. . . .

The time between Pac Rim and the Olympic Trials in July turned out to be very stressful for me. I had strained a muscle in my leg—not the leg I'd had surgery on, the other one. When I told the trainers it was bothering me, they suggested I take a week off to rest it. They believed time off from doing leg conditioning and running would help. So I did exactly what they said and still did bars and light beam work, and I didn't tumble or exert my lower body. But after a week it hurt even more, which confused me. I kept thinking, *It's just a muscle strain—I don't understand why it could possibly feel this bad.* But the muscle wasn't firing up properly, so I knew that in both upcoming competitions—the Secret Classic in Hartford, Connecticut, and the P&Gs in St. Louis—I would have to work around the strain, if I could compete at all.

Now, I'm a mentally strong individual. Throughout my recovery from the earlier wrist and knee injuries, I proved my strength to others and to myself. I refused to accept defeat. I might have been stressed at first, but I got motivated quickly and did the job I had to in order to get better. But for some reason, I just couldn't understand how this latest strain wasn't getting better. I was super frustrated.

One night, right after I returned from Pac Rim, my family took me out to dinner at one of my favorite Tex-Mex restaurants. It's called Freppe's, and it's owned by Jelysa's boyfriend, Joe Deserio. Suddenly, out of nowhere, even before we got through the nachos, I started having a total meltdown. I don't know what came over me, I just started hysterically crying. At first everyone was shocked into silence because I almost never cry. I get nervous, but I usually don't do tears. That night, though, I remember saying between sobs, "I don't know if I can do this anymore. I don't think my body can take it."

When I looked up, everyone's shocked expressions seemed to say, *Who is this person? Give us back our Laurie.* Then they all came together and said things like "Look, this gift you have for gymnastics was given to you because it's meant to be your platform." "Now is your time, you even said so yourself!" "You're such a talented girl. You've worked so hard. You have to keep going." "If anybody can do it, you can!" They all promised to continue to be there for me, and I know they meant it, but I still couldn't stop crying. That's when Jelysa said, "I get it. This is beyond anything any of us have ever done. I totally would have quit by now, but you're not a quitter. That's not who you are. I've always known you to be passionate and to keep going even when other people just give up."

Somehow, that got through to me. I heard what she was saying, and my crying slowed until it was just sniffles. The waitresses kept giving me tissues the whole time, so by the end of the meal I had this mound of used Kleenex piled in front of me. Jelysa reached across the table and grabbed them. "Give me those," she said. She stuffed them in her pocket, and as we were leaving, she told my dad she wasn't throwing them away. She said she was keeping them so that when I made the Olympic team, she could give them back to me as a reminder of my struggle and of this defining moment. She knew that if I was crying, I had to be going through something much tougher than they ever imagined, because I just never show that kind of stress. I'm a gymnast, and gymnasts are used to holding all of that in. (Well, there was that time in the very beginning when I got my first rip and I thought the world was going to end, but I'm a lot tougher now!) If the caption under Marcus's Facebook picture on his prom night was proof of his belief in me, collecting all those tissues that evening was Jelysa's *I know she's going to make it* moment.

I used my family's pep talk as fuel to help me get through the next few competitions. I think it was because they were the right words, said at the right time, in the right way. When injuries occur, it's usually because your body is trying to tell you something. The message might be, *You're doing this thing all wrong* or *You're driving yourself too hard.* But in competitive environments, people are constantly telling you to push through the pain, and that message can drown out what your body is saying and what your body needs. In gymnastics, part of it is that the window of opportunity is pretty narrow. I was reminded of that fact a lot during my injuries. Although my newest injury didn't seem as bad as the earlier ones, it would still need time to heal, and that window-of-opportunity thing was lurking in the back of my mind, making me feel like time was running out. The Olympics were just three months away, so that voice—the one telling me to push through the pain—was more insistent than usual. All of this together was what had brought on my meltdown. But what I heard Jelysa saying was, *We believe in you. You're so close. Take it one step at a time, but don't give up, because you've worked too hard to get here.* And those words resonated deeply with me. They were exactly what I needed to get me over and through.

When the strain lingered for a couple more weeks, I began questioning if I'd have enough time to prepare for the Olympics. I got therapy for it, and acupuncture treatments, too, but when they didn't work, I ultimately saw Dr. Scott Greenberg, who's treated many other Olympic athletes with complex injuries. That's when we realized how serious the strain was. My VMO muscle, located just above and to the inside of my knee, was badly damaged. Luckily, Dr. Greenberg is known for repairing this kind of injury using an amazing treatment called PRP (which stands for platelet-rich plasma). Basically, he took platelets and other growth factors from my own blood and injected them right into the area where my damaged muscle wasn't healing properly, thereby helping my body to heal itself. I couldn't believe it! In seven weeks, I went from being unable to bend my knee to beating Dr. Greenberg in a high-jump competition on the clinic's patient beds! Once again I found myself so grateful that I'd persevered and that I'd gotten the kind of excellent medical care I needed. Now it was time to get back to competing and making it to the Olympics.

TRIALS AND TRIBULATIONS

CHAPTER 11

IN JUNE, I HEADED TO HARTFORD TO COMPETE IN the Secret Classic, but I only did bars there because we wanted to avoid stressing my knee too much. Mostly, the team management needed to see if I could compete—they were clearly looking ahead to determine my potential for the Olympics and whether I could still physically withstand the pressures.

As it turned out, I scored a 15.400 and everyone was happy with that—most of all me. Even though I didn't compete in all four events at the Classic, I still qualified for the P&Gs later that month.

The P&G Championships are often held in different

host cities, but this time they were in St. Louis again. St. Louis, as you will recall, was where my mom first taught me to celebrate my disappointments after I came in twenty-first place all those years ago. It was heartwarming to return to the city knowing that this time, I was on the brink of making the US Olympic team. Though I did have to keep things real, because that still wasn't a sure thing. How I did at the P&Gs would determine whether I got to the Trials, and how I did at the Trials would determine if I went to the Olympics.

At the end of day one of the two-day competition, Simone came in first and I was tied for second with Aly in the all-around. She and I both had a score of 60.450. But after the full competition scores were totaled on day two, Simone had won the all-around, Aly had come in second, and I had taken third. I also placed third on bars and beam and tied for third with MyKayla Skinner on floor. Although Aly and I had jostled for second on the all-around, and she had ultimately won, I was content. My mission had been to make it to the Olympic Trials, and I had done that.

My goal for the Trials was basically the same as what my goal had been for the P&Gs: I had to show Marta and all the other Olympic staff that they could trust me enough to put me up in Rio. So my whole agenda coming into those Trials was to hit all my routines. During practice, I kept thinking about every possible thing that could mess me up. I had to go back to my earliest training and remember how to quiet those thoughts in my head. I had to focus on technique, technique, technique.

On the day of the Trials, which took place in San Jose, California, all the girls were crying. I think Aly started it because, at age twenty-two, this could be her last Olympic Trials. Once she started crying, Simone started crying, and then I started crying. It was a whole thing, and that's when all the girls competing kind of huddled up and one of the gymnasts, Amelia Hundley, said, "You know what, guys? No matter what happens, we all love each other. Just because one of us doesn't get named to the team, that doesn't mean we're bad students; it just means it wasn't our time." Throughout the whole final stretch of that season, we'd all been so supportive of each other. When we'd been backstage at the P&Gs, everyone was nervous. It had been a stressful year for a lot of us, so we were giving each other hugs on hugs on hugs. That's when Brenna Dowell, who was competing, too, suggested that we pray together quickly before the start of the meet. We all got into a circle, held hands, and asked that we be kept safe, that we have a great time that day, and that we all just be there for each other. That moment at the P&Gs—and the moment just before the

Trials when we huddled together the way we did—were two of the best ways ever to start a competition.

Thankfully, in the end I did hit all my routines at the Olympic Trials! There was only one exception. On the second day, I stepped out of bounds on floor. That was a stressful moment, but it was a small enough mistake, and I'd otherwise executed such a strong routine, I knew my chances weren't over as long as I was very careful for the other three events. Still, I'm sure I gave my parents a heart attack. The anxiety was crazy the whole time, and you could feel the tension in the air. Ultimately, I ended up placing second in the all-around behind Simone, and I made the team!!!

Simone Biles, Gabby Douglas, Aly Raisman, Madison Kocian, and I were going to the Olympics to represent the United States of America in women's gymnastics, and I couldn't have been more ecstatic! That moment confirmed just how strong we all were. I felt like we were superheroes. I remember stripping down my warm-ups and putting on the USA warm-ups. They were blue, which I think of as a power color. We were handed flowers and there was confetti everywhere. We were no longer individuals competing against each other: we were a team.

The night before I was flying to Texas to begin practicing with the new official team, my family held a going-away party for me. Coincidentally, it was at the same restaurant where I'd my tearful meltdown after the Pacific Rim competition. This time, though, I was much cheerier and it was Jelysa who got emotional.

She pulled out this bag of goodies and handed it to me. I noticed she had tears in her eyes and I thought, *I know I'm leaving and I know you love me, but jeez.* She coaxed me to look inside the bag. That's when I saw this cute little purse. She said, "Open it!" Inside, there were tissues, and for the life of me I couldn't understand why. Then she explained that these tissues had stayed in her coat pocket all season long. They were the ones she'd taken from me the night of my meltdown, and she'd saved them for this very occasion to mark my journey from that moment to this one. She wanted me to know that all along she'd had faith in me. I was so moved, I almost started crying *again*!

After I had a delicious quesadilla (what else?!), Marcus drove me home early because I always need my sleep. We talked about all the adversity leading up to the Trials and how I'd gotten through it. That three-month rough patch was really the only time I'd had doubts about whether I was going to make it. The thing about those doubts, though, is that they weren't just surface doubts. I'd wondered during that time if it might be all over for me. Not just as an Olympic hopeful, but as a competitive gymnast in general.

Besides having to live with all my own uncertainty during that period, I'd also had to face something new: fans openly expressing their own concerns about me. I'd read a few comments on Tumblr about how I was nice and all, but how I wasn't ready for the Olympics. I think a lot of people just didn't know enough about me then. While I was known by decision makers and other competitors in the gymnastics world, gymnastics fans are generally more in tune with the senior members of the team, and I had only become a senior that year. There were so many seniors whose careers up until that point made them viable contenders. The media focused on them because it didn't seem like anyone else would break through the pack. I was a dark horse going into Trials. In the weeks leading up, some of the girls who the media assumed would make the team were already on magazine covers and even had endorsement deals and commercials. In some cases, the media guessed incorrectly. For instance, they thought Maggie Nichols was going, and when she didn't because of an injury, I'm sure it was heartbreaking for her. Maggie had torn the meniscus in her knee right before Pacific Rim and needed surgery to repair it. I was inspired by how hard she worked to get back in shape, but there just wasn't enough time. She is someone I've always looked up to as a phenomenal gymnast and an awesome team leader. And most of all, I admired the way she handled her disappointment with such dignity and grace.

Looking back, I probably focused a little too much on all the speculation about who was going and who wasn't. Other people may have thought I was a long shot, but I didn't think so, and that's what mattered. I did what I always do when there's an obstacle in front of me: I just held my head up and kept going until I finally reached my destination. I used all that crazy emotion as motivation. I thought, *Oh, you don't think I'm ready? I'll show you!* And I did show them.

I must say that making the Olympic team was not only a personal victory for me. My coach, Maggie, had never gone to the Olympics before, either. I was her first elite gymnast, her first National Team member, her first gymnast to compete internationally—and now I was her first gymnast going to the Olympics. For more than a decade we'd worked together. And most of all, we had grown together. That was something great about us. Because competing in the Olympics is such an incredible honor and because we were both able go there for the first time together, we both knew this moment was one we'd remember forever.

RIO!

CHAPTER 12

AFTER ELEVEN LONG YEARS OF TRAINING FOR THE Olympics, it was crazy how fast everything happened next.

Because the media hadn't been positioning me as one of the five team members leading into the Trials, my family hadn't allowed themselves to consider the possibility of a trip to Rio. Then the announcement came that I was going, and suddenly they were going to have to scurry for last-minute plane tickets and pack their bags. I was already on my way to Texas for Olympic training camp when my family sat down and talked about who would go with me. It was decided that only my parents would head to Brazil—because the threat of the Zika virus was so serious, all adult family members of childbearing age were advised to stay home. (Honestly, I didn't even consider Zika in relation to myself. As far as I was concerned, this was a once- or twice-in-a-lifetime opportunity, and it was something I definitely didn't want to miss. I can't think of anything that could have stopped me from going!) Since Jelysa was twenty-seven and Marcus was twenty, and since someone needed to stay home to care for my elderly grandmother, it made sense that they both remained behind. At first I was disappointed, but then I realized they'd been watching many of my competitions from a distance all these years, and yet I still always felt their presence. Besides, my parents deserved to have a vacation all by themselves!

Rio was so crowded, my parents ended up staying at a hotel an hour away from the Olympic Village. Even though there were news reports of crime and robberies at Ipanema Beach and concerns about the quality of the water, both my mother and father thought Brazil was a beautiful country. What my dad always tells people is, "It was a great trip. I didn't get robbed. I didn't catch Zika. And my daughter came home with two medals!" I kind of think that says it all.

I didn't see my mom or dad until after the Olympics

were over, because the rules for our team were strict. That was okay with me, though. It enabled them to actually enjoy the festivities on their own—and besides, I was really busy practicing and bonding with the girls. We arrived in Rio about a week before the Games started, and we all stayed together in an apartment building in the Olympic Village that housed all the US teams. Many countries had their own building where their athletes stayed; China had its own building, Japan had its own building, and so on. There were a lot of levels to our building. We were located on the third floor, and I think Michael Phelps was on one of the top floors. Our apartment was really nice. It had a little family-style living room, and then there were two tables set up so we could get physical therapy and treatment after our workouts. It was great that our trainers and nurses traveled with us. Simone and I slept in one bedroom, Maddy and Aly slept in the other, and Gabby had her own room since that room had only one bed.

Although there were buses available so the athletes could get around Rio to sightsee, our team really didn't travel anywhere outside the Olympic Village. We understood that the team management wanted us to remain extremely focused. The kind of structure they set up helped guarantee that our attention remained solely on the Olympics and the job we had to do—there was no room for any distractions. It's why we didn't go the opening ceremonies. Marta wanted us to remain sharp and conserve our energy. There is a lot going on during the ceremonies, and while they are entertaining and exhilarating, they last so long that they can be draining. Getting rest and settling into our schedule and our new environment mattered more than participating in all the early celebrations. We wanted to be prepared to give our very best when it was our turn to perform for the world!

During the whole time we were in Rio, whenever we went to practice, we all walked together. Even when we went to lunch, we all walked together. And the coaches and staff walked with us, too—I don't think we ever traveled without Marta or our staff accompanying us. I actually liked when we walked the sidewalks as a group, checking out the streets lined with the flags from other countries. It was beautiful. And everyone was out: not just gymnasts and not just the USA team members, but lots of athletes from lots of different countries and sports. There were random bikers and speed-walkers, too. We all said hi to each other or nodded and smiled. There were no social barriers, even though we were from different nations and were there to compete.

In addition to our apartment and where we practiced, we also spent a lot of time in the cafeteria. It was clear that as the host nation, Brazil tried to accommodate everyone's needs and tastes. There was American food on one side, Asian food on the other, and Spanish food, too. They even had special meals in case you had a dairy allergy or some other food restriction. After we ate, we'd go around to talk with the athletes from the other countries to see where they were from and what they did. Everyone was very friendly. And I couldn't believe all the different kinds of figures we saw. Athletes come in every shape and size! There were some who were extremely muscular because they're weight lifters. Then there were the ones who were extremely lean because they run marathons. One day we met these volleyball players who were all over seven feet tall! We laughed because they were just towering over us.

Another thing the girls and I loved to do was trade pins. It was something we'd done before at international competitions, but it was especially fun at the Olympics. The staff gave us a ton of USA pins and we'd go up to athletes from other countries and exchange one of ours for one of theirs. I probably have fifty or sixty pins from other countries, and they're something I'll hang on to forever. These pin exchanges were a great way to break the ice and start a conversation. My parents speak Spanish fluently and I'm studying it now, but I still didn't have the skills to hold conversations with the Spanish-speaking athletes. When I look back, I think I probably missed a great opportunity to practice with them! But I couldn't believe how many of the people we talked to understood English. And even when they didn't, we had these lanyards with our credentials and our official pin on them. So we just held those out and pointed to the pin. When the other athlete saw that, it was as if they automatically knew to trade them with us.

In the end, I didn't mind having to stay within the confines of the Olympic Village. It was amazing to see and meet all these people from around the world who came together for the love of their sport.

STRIKING GOLD

CHAPTER 13

SOMETHING THAT ALWAYS CONFUSES PEOPLE about the women's gymnastics competition at the Olympics is the way the qualification round works. Learning the rules is tricky, but not nearly as tricky as, say, learning to do "the Biles"—that crazy move Simone does when she follows two backflips with a half twist. So just hang in there with me while I give you a crash course on the qualification round, because believe it or not, it's one of the most important parts of the Olympics.

Basically, qualifications (or "prelims," as we sometimes call them) determine who moves on to each of the three different final events: team finals, all-around finals, and individual event finals. To move on to *team finals*, four team members from each nation compete in all four key events: vault, bars, beam, and floor. (By the way, the group of four gymnasts does not have to be the same for every event. Since there are five team members in total, you can mix and match the group so the gymnasts with the strongest skills in a specific event get to compete in that event.) The three top scores for each event count toward the overall team score. The eight top-scoring teams move on to the team finals.

If you are one of the twenty-four top-scoring athletes during qualifications, you get to move on to the *all-around finals*, where, by competing on every apparatus—vault, bars, beam, and floor—the all-around best athlete in the sport is determined. But there is a catch: only two athletes from each country can move on to compete in the all-around! (Keep that fact in mind because it will be important later on.) The goal behind this rule—just like at the international events—is to prevent a single nation from dominating an event and competing largely against themselves.

If you are one of eight top-scoring athletes in one of the apparatus events during qualifications, then you get to move on and compete for an *individual* finals title for that apparatus. For instance, if you were one of the eight best-performing gymnasts on vault, you would get to compete against the other seven top-performing gymnasts on vault for the gold, silver, or bronze medal for vault. But no more than two individuals per country are selected in the top eight for individual finals competition. Of course, the gymnast who scores the highest in each individual event moves on to compete in the individual finals.

The reason the qualifications are so important is that if your team isn't one of the top eight to make it, then your only chance to medal at the Olympics at all will be to compete as an individual—and you have to score high enough at the qualifications to move on to the individual finals. You are always trying to earn a spot in the finals for the team as well as for yourself.

Thankfully, before we even started practice for the Olympics, we sensed how stressful this competition was going to be and we came to the same conclusion: no one can do it alone. If you even try to go it alone, the weight and enormity of it will mess with you. We knew we were all in this thing together, so we had to support each other no matter what. For that reason, no one one-upped each other in practice. We were always cheering for each other, saying, "Come on, Maddy, you can do it!" or "Don't give up, Simone!" Our mutual goal was to help each other remain confident so we could all do our best.

At this level of competition, there is definitely a part

of you that's competing against yourself and your previous performances. All the other girls had been to the world championships before and won medals, so they knew what events and milestones they were going for. In many ways we were each just trying to improve our prior bests. I knew at the very least I wanted to make it to the team final. And, of course, we *all* wanted to win team gold.

In the end, the qualifications went really well for us.

Aly, Simone, Gabby, and I started off competing in floor. I was the first to go, which is one of my pet peeves. I really hate going first or last because my nerves are always worse on either end of an event. But I had to get used to it because I was also first on vault.

Aly and Gabby had been to the Olympics before, so one piece of advice they gave me was to enjoy the experience, because when you're out there, your body goes on autopilot. You've done your routine so many times already, your muscle memory naturally takes over. So you really have to do your best to have fun in the moment, because before you know it, you blink and your routine is over.

I got us off to a good start. Simone came in first with a score of 15.733; Aly came in second with a score of 15.275; I came in third with a 14.800; and Gabby came in fourth with a score of 14.366. Next, Gabby, Simone,

Aly, and I did vault, which helped loosen us up because it was something most of us simply had to get out of the way—only Simone could qualify for vault finals. For that particular apparatus, you need two vaults in a family, meaning that each vault needs to start out differently than the other. She was the only one with that skill, so we all had to rely on her for this event.

It's helpful to know that the scoring process for vault is a little different than for the other events, as the two vault scores are averaged together. All I can say is that Simone's scores were ridiculously good. She got a 16.000! Everybody was so proud of her. It was an amazing moment.

After that event, Maddy, Aly, Simone, and Gabby did bars.

Remember that pesky rule in the Olympic guidelines I told you about? The one where only two athletes from the same country can compete in the all-around finals? Well, someone had to sit out the bars event during qualifications, and whoever that person ended up being would lose their shot at winning the all-around, too. It was either Aly or me who would miss out this time, because Simone had already secured the number one spot; Maddy was our bars specialist, so she had to compete; and Gabby, who was the defending Olympic champion of the all-around, was also strong on bars.

As it turned out, Aly's solid performance during podium training factored heavily into Marta's decision about who would compete. And having a small muscle strain in my stomach didn't help me. We were very discreet about my injury because we hoped it would improve quickly. But the strain was a little too unpredictable. One day it would be fine, and the next it would hurt badly. The muscle was in my core, which is something you work in every event, so it wasn't an injury to risk aggravating.

At first, I was really disappointed when I was chosen to sit out, because bars and the all-around were events I thought I could have scored really well in. But I calmed myself down and remembered to celebrate the fact that I was, you know, at the Olympics at all. Some earlier life lessons started to come back to me: if being in the all-around wasn't right for me at this time, I would be directed to something that was. Then I was able to feel extremely grateful that I was able to compete in the three other events. Who knows? If I had been able to do bars that day, my stomach might have gotten worse and I wouldn't have been able to compete in beam.

The good news is that Maddy killed it on bars. We were all hoping she'd come in first place, and of course, she delivered. She handled that event with so much ease and grace. She scored a 15.866. Gabby came in close behind her, taking third place with a score of 15.766.

They both qualified for the bars final.

Finally, Simone, Gabby, Aly, and I competed on beam. Simone finished first with a score of 15.633. I came in second with a 15.366. Aly and Gabby tied for seventh with a 14.833 score. So both Simone and I headed into the beam finals from there!

It was completely awesome: Team USA not only placed first among all eight qualifying teams, making it into the team and all-around finals, but every member of our team qualified for at least one individual final, too! It was the first time in a long time something like that had happened. Aly explained to us how rare this was: When only four out of five team members can compete in each of the events in the qualifying rounds, the odds are that at least one person is not going to get a shot at an individual event. We totally beat the odds!

We were all so giddy and excited. We could be happy for all of us as a group, not just ourselves individually. Even when you're expected to succeed because the USA team has consistently been such a strong team, it's still surprising and thrilling and unbelievable all at once. Everybody could feel the energy around us.

The amazing thing about the Olympics is that you feel so many different emotions in the span of a few days, and they are all intense. So it was nice to have at least one totally playful moment. For me that moment happened during my floor routine in the team finals, just before we won. I spontaneously winked at one of the judges and everyone there, and at home, seemed to love that. But honestly I don't know what came over me. Right before I went on, I was so nervous I looked at the team and said, "Guys, I'm so scared. It's the last event, what if I mess up?" Any time you are competing as a team you have those worries—I know I had certainly felt the same way at international meets. Thankfully, the girls assured me that wasn't going to happen. They said, "No, no, no, you're fine. Don't worry about it. We're a few points ahead, so just go out there and enjoy yourself."

I made my way toward the warm-up area. I was feeling pretty good by then, so I stood to the side and took a deep breath. I wanted to soak in everything around me, because it was definitely a major moment. I scanned the cheering crowd and all I saw was a sea of green. Brazil's colors are yellow, blue, and green, and the entire arena was decked out in green. The mats were green, the logos were green, everything around me was green, and for a split second, I found it kind of intimidating because in the United States, all our equipment is blue. Even a seemingly small difference like that can be jarring.

Then all of a sudden I heard this beep. It was coming from the little TV screen in the warm-up area that lists your name, your country, and the event you're about to compete in. My screen read *Lauren Hernandez, USA, Floor Exercise*. After I heard the beep, the screen switched to *GO*, which meant I had to go salute the judges and begin.

When I stood up on the floor, I could see one of the out-of-bounds judges in my line of vision. That is the judge who checks to make sure your foot never crosses over the white line. Well, I looked straight at her and suddenly felt this surge of confidence to wink. After I did that, I went on to do an amazing routine. When it was done, I was so proud of myself! Later, a woman came up to me while I was watching Simone and Aly compete in their all-around finals and she said, "Wow, I just want you to know that when you winked at the judge, it really worked." I didn't know how to respond, so I just said, "Thank you. That's very nice of you to say." That's when she told me she was the out-of-bounds judge! All I could say was "Oh my goodness."

That was a great moment, but probably the most epic moment of all was standing on the podium with my teammates to receive our gold medals later that day. During the four events in the team finals, we executed twelve hit routines and took first place, winning the gold medal eight points ahead of Russia, who came in second to earn a silver medal, followed by China, who earned the bronze medal. We were the third women's gymnastics team in USA history—in addition to the 1996 and 2012 teams—to win gold in the team finals!

At one point after the medal was around my neck and I was taking in everything it meant, I searched the crowd for my parents. Everyone around them was congratulating them, and my dad was beaming with pride. I waited for them to look at me: in a crowd of all those people, I wanted to be sure to share the moment with them, because they'd given so much to make sure I got there.

After it was over, when someone asked my dad what he was feeling, he said, "Everything," and then after a beat he said, "And nothing." That pretty much describes the feeling: You are so full of emotion, everything stops for a moment so you can take it all in. And then you are numb from the reality of it. I'd caught sight of my parents at an earlier point in the day, too, and I'd had this fleeting thought that makes me smile even when I think about it now. I was walking from floor to beam and I was trying to spot them, but I didn't want to be obvious about it. I still had to keep my head in the competition. When I saw them, I thought, *Wow, I'm here. You're here. Wait, we're all here together.* It was like I was checking my mental GPS to be sure we were not only where we were, but that we were there experiencing this totally awesome thing together. My parents never got to go to any of my international competitions—they'd always had to

Livestream them—so it really was euphoric to have them there in Rio with me.

After team finals, we killed it in the all-around finals, too. Simone came in first, earning a gold medal, and Aly came in second, earning a silver medal, while Russia's Aliya Mustafina came in third, earning a bronze medal. It was amazing. The first and second all-around best gymnasts in the world are now both Americans. That hasn't happened since Shawn Johnson and Nastia Liukin locked in both titles at the 2008 Olympics in Beijing. And here's the wild thing: if Aly hadn't competed on bars, that might not have happened at all. In many ways, it proves my philosophy. On that day, Aly was on the path that was intended for her. That realization made me feel a lot better about having to sit out bars.

As for the individual finals, the USA women's gymnastics team took home six more medals: Simone won gold for vault and floor, and bronze for beam; Maddy won silver for bars; Aly won silver for floor; and I won silver on beam. I'm thrilled to say I hit every skill in my routine. I felt especially great about how I came out from my punch front pike with my chest up high at the very beginning. I was in the zone during each of my leaps, and I felt the crowd with me. But it all went so quickly! Before I knew it, I was dismounting. All I'd had to do was land cleanly with a round-off double pike, and I did. I think that was one of the best routines I showed in Rio. I was happy I performed the way I had in practice—my mission was accomplished.

When I think back on the Olympics, there were only two times I was anxious for myself or for one of my teammates. In my beam routine, I always find the triple series (or what is called a flight series) a little nerve-racking. That's when I have to perform three moves in a row backward: I do a back handspring, followed by a layout step-out, followed by another layout step-out. I had a good feeling before I was going to compete that I would hit it, but it's something I'm always slightly worried about in the back of my mind. The other thing that had me holding my breath was Aly's first tumble, because she does so much in that pass. I don't think she's ever worried about it, because in her head she's doing everything she needs to do to execute it beautifully. But as you watch, there's a lot going on, so you fear something might go wrong. She basically does a round-off, a backward one-and-a-half twist, and then she steps out of that to connect to another round-off, a back handspring, and then she does this spring called a double Arabian and basically goes up in the air to do a half turn and double front flip connected to a front layout, which is a front flip with a straight leg where her whole body is open. It's incredible! It's so insane. It wows me every single time.

Once she gets past that, we know the rest of her routine is fine. And she ends up nailing it every single time.

All up, our team won nine medals, breaking the all-time record formerly shared by the 1984 and 2008 teams. It felt so good to be strong, to be able to come together, to do what we know how to do, and to get such great results from the effort. We were on top of the world—and very ready for a pizza party.

THE FINAL FIVE

CHAPTER 14

I'VE ALWAYS LOVED THE GYMNASTICS TRADITION
of naming the Olympic team. If you look back, you'll see
that the moniker each team picked really fit their personality as a group.

In 1996, there were seven members on the team—
Kerri Strug, Shannon Miller, Dominique Dawes,
Dominique Moceanu, Amanda Borden, Jaycie Phelps,
and Amy Chow—and they were all really magnificent.
You know they came up with the name the Magnificent Seven because at the time they believed they would
become the first US women's gymnastics team to win
gold in the team finals. The Olympics were in Atlanta,

Georgia, that year, so it was even more magnificent to have accomplished it in their home country.

In 2012, before the team went to London, the media dubbed them the Fab Five because they were a very sassy, glamorous group. McKayla Maroney, Kyla Ross, and Jordyn Wieber were on the team, in addition to Gabby and Aly. But there was already a group of male college basketball players from the nineties known as the Fab Five, so when the girls got a chance to pick their own name, they chose the Fierce Five to show how determined they were to bring home the second team gold in history for the women's gymnastics team. Of course, Gabby was particularly fierce, bringing home the gold in the all-around final. At the time, I watched those gymnasts and was so inspired by them! I thought the name suited them then and I still do.

When I think about our team name, I can't imagine calling ourselves anything other than the Final Five. It fits us perfectly: it's both dramatic and touching, reflecting not only the fact that we're the last team of five members who will compete in the Olympics (in 2020 the team size will shrink to four members and possibly two specialists), but also our admiration for Marta Karolyi, who announced her retirement before we headed to Brazil. Each of our careers has been incredibly affected by Marta, and her legacy to the sport and to the world is huge. Over several decades she mentored and developed some of the most talented gymnasts and coaches that artistic gymnastics has ever known. Her formula—three routines on beam, one routine on floor, three routines on vault, and two routines on bars—is what we followed in every single workout, every single day, again and again and again. It never changed. That strategy created the consistency each one of us needed in order to succeed. She would tailor the workouts to our individual strengths and weaknesses, and that's how she developed teammates who complemented each other. Her workouts were exhausting, we'd all tell you that. It was very hard to get a day off from her; you'd have to be sick or injured for that to happen. But we didn't mind, because we always knew she wanted the best for us. She was very strict, but we respected her for it. And all that work showed in our skills. When we came up with our name, we just wanted to find a special way to say thank you.

Although we picked the name over group text right after the Olympic Trials, we tried to keep it a secret until just the right time. We were all texting back and forth that day, trying to think of something powerful, and if I remember correctly, it was Simone who came up with it. I can't even recall the other suggestions, because we all knew that was the one as soon as we heard it. All throughout prelims and team finals, whenever we would huddle to show that we were a team and that we were there for each other, we'd put our hands together and shout, "Go USA!" But as soon as we knew we'd won the gold medal as a team, we changed things up in our next huddle and shouted, "We are the Final Five!" We waved to the crowd and then made our way over to the coaches and to Marta. We gave her hugs and asked, "Did you hear our team name?" She said, "No, what was it?" When we told her it was the Final Five, she put her hands to her face and we saw tears in her eyes. It was cute. Marta's super tough and doesn't show that kind of emotion, so it was especially heartwarming to know our choice moved her like that.

In the end, I think the name not only marks the transition from one era to the next, but it also reflects the team's gratitude. We appreciate the opportunities we've been given—we all have different personalities, but that is one of the traits we share. And it has created this incredible sense that we're a family, now and forever. These girls, whom I've gotten to know inside and out, mean the world to me.

Before the Olympics, I didn't know Maddy well. She was always the shy one. We'd say "Hi, how are you?" whenever we saw each other, and maybe we'd share a laugh when something funny happened, but she was always quiet. We were both so focused on our workouts, too, that we didn't spend a lot of time developing a friendship. But once we made the Olympic team and had more time together, we both had the same thought: *Hey, she's really cool.* Suddenly, there was this spark of a friendship. Maybe we grew closer because we were together so much, but sometimes I think the Maddy I know now is not the Maddy she was when I first met her. She went from being kind of reserved to being a total jokester, and that playful quality draws me to her. Whenever we were in meetings or had to give an interview as a group, we'd all be a little nervous. It doesn't matter how many times you do those kinds of things, you still get butterflies. And it was always Maddy who would say something funny or positive to break the tension. I never would have thought that about her a year ago, and I'm so happy we've gotten to know each other well and we've had amazing experiences together.

I love Aly, too. By now I think everyone knows we call her Grams, short for Grandma. It's because the girl can never get enough sleep! Even after she wakes up, she's ready for a nap. She will literally set her alarm to get up in the morning, go to breakfast, and then come back and say, "Okay, guys. Don't bother me. I'm gonna go take a nap." And it would only be eleven o'clock in the morning! I couldn't believe it the first time it happened. We all looked at each other like, *Are you serious?* She also has the biggest heart. She's the perfect team captain because she is very motherly—her other nickname is Mama Aly for that reason. It's not just because she's the oldest, it's because she cares about us and always wants to make sure we're okay. Every so often she'd ask, "Did you eat well today?" Or if one of us was still sleeping when all the others were already up and getting ready, she'd come into our room and make sure we were awake. She's also been known to tuck me into bed and kiss me good night. She's so cute! I respect how hard she works, too. She has one of the best work ethics ever.

Although I thought Maddy was the shy one at first, it's actually Gabby who's kind of quiet. I know that's surprising, but it's true. Even so, she's hilarious. Whenever we were in a situation where we couldn't say what we were feeling, she would purposely look our way with a mischievous twinkle in her eye. It was as if she was telling us the funniest joke without even using words. For instance, if we found out that practice was starting earlier than usual or we had to stay late, she would flash us that look and we'd know she was thinking the same exact thing we were, only she would make us giggle instead of groan about it. It was like she could do stand-up comedy through telepathy. All five of us would practically fall down laughing, and no one else had a clue why. Aside from being so much fun, Gabby is also one of the nicest people I know. Whenever we were stressing out, she would jump in and give us a jolt of confidence, saying, "That's all right, girls. You got it. You got it." She always managed to help ease our anxiety.

Aly could probably testify best as to how well Simone and I get along. We were in the same room during the Olympics, and we were a ton of trouble. Once competition was done, Aly would have to bang on our door at night for us to keep quiet so she could sleep. But Simone and I would just keep giggling. We'd stay up till all hours, playing lots of music, jumping on the beds, dancing around, and ordering room service constantly. We're so close and we think so much alike, sometimes I wonder if this is what being twins feels like. It was funny, because once during the Olympics there was a fire drill in the middle of the night and everyone was rushing to get out the door, but Simone and I had the same exact thought: *Our medals! We've got to get our medals!* We were running around in such a tizzy trying to collect them all. What I love most about Simone is that she doesn't only make me laugh, she's the one making everyone else laugh, too. You just have to hear her giggle and it makes you giggle. You don't even have to know what the joke is, that's how infectious her laugh is. Even if you're having a rough day, she can absolutely turn it around. I feel like Simone and I just have this amazing chemistry. I don't know if I've ever had that with any other friend. She totally cracks me up. Even as I'm writing this, I have a big grin on my face.

Seriously, though, I went into the Olympics with one sister and somehow I came home with four more. I will always feel a special bond with the Final Five. Always.

ON PARADE

CHAPTER 15

WHEN I CAME HOME FROM THE OLYMPICS, MY hometown of Old Bridge held a huge parade for me. I didn't know what to expect, but I certainly didn't think thousands of people would come out and cheer for me.

I was in this motorcade that wound through the streets and ended up at Lombardi Field on the grounds of Carl Sandburg Middle School. I sat on top of a black Mustang, and as I was waving and smiling, I was overwhelmed by the fact that all of this was for me. Even when I think about it now, I'm kind of speechless. So many little kids, so many teenagers, and so many adults poured out of their homes to say hello. Some of them ran up to the car and dropped off bouquets of flowers. It was so sweet! Then, at the school, there was this carnival with lots of food, games, and activities. All the school's gymnasts were there. Some of the little girls from my gym came, too, and of course, Shannon, Paloma, and my good friend Emily Liszewski were there. My teammate Riley McCusker was also kind enough to drive down from Connecticut to celebrate with me. But it was the faces of all the people who I didn't know, who were genuinely happy for me, that blew me away. I hope some of them were thinking, *Someday, this could happen to me, too.* It was just so crazy to see all the support and love that people had for the Olympics, for gymnastics, and for me. I had goose bumps the entire day. All the time I was involved in the sport up until that point, I had never realized how many people at home were watching me and rooting for my success. I was so focused on my training, to me it was just what I needed to do to succeed. But for so many people, it was much more than that.

Because Marcus and Jelysa had stayed home during the Olympics, in many ways, they had already experienced some of the local excitement and appreciation in the air. People had expressed their excitement for me when they saw my brother and sister at church or at the supermarket. But my siblings had actually decided to watch the events at home by themselves. I know that sounds strange, since everyone thinks it's a great idea to have viewing parties. But they didn't want people to see their emotional reactions, or their reactions if they disagreed with the judges. They know that I always respect the judges' calls—after all, they're doing their best in the moment, the same way all the gymnasts are doing their best in the moment—but it can still be hard if you see things differently than the judges do. A few friends had stopped by to see my siblings here and there during the Olympics, but they knew my brother and sister watched my competitions with a different kind of investment than anyone else. Jelysa and Marcus tend to hang on my every little move. They know my routines so well, they can see when I hit a skill and when I don't. And even if I do hit it, they can see where I've executed something with more or less confidence or precision than usual. They're not just looking at the overall outcome, they're looking at each nanosecond. They clench each other's hands, tear up at times, and then pump their fists in the air at other times.

On the night I won the silver medal, however, they did decide to watch from Joe's restaurant, where ESPN was covering the event. And it ended up being one of the greatest nights of their lives, too. From what they told me, all of New Jersey's heart was with me that evening. They had so much fun and felt so much pride, I'm not sure they'll choose to be alone watching me compete ever again!

Although my grandmother couldn't stay up late enough to watch the Olympics, Jelysa and Marcus showed her clips on their phones. I'm the baby of the family and I definitely held a special place in her heart, so she was very proud and amazed to see me do what I do. But the seriousness of my accomplishment didn't really hit her until she saw it on Spanish TV!

In addition to this outpouring of love from my hometown and family, the media had great affection for me, too. They seemed to love my playfulness and confidence, and throughout the Olympics they called me "sassy" and "cheeky." They also added a few new nicknames to the ones I already went by (my family sometimes calls me Monkey because of my love for swinging from the uneven bars, and from anything else I could practice on, as a little kid). Now the media was calling me the Human Emoji, and they even revived the nickname "Baby Shakira" that sports commentator Jessica O'Beirne had coined a few years earlier (because she thought I moved like the singer in my floor routines and because I share Shakira's Latin heritage). I loved it! It made me so happy that people were acknowledging my bubbly personality as much as my skills, because at the core, that's who I really am.

I'm also incredibly proud of my Puerto Rican heritage, but at first I wasn't sure why everyone was talking about it. Then I realized that as I was growing up, there hadn't been any Latina role models in gymnastics! I asked my parents if they could think of any, and we ended up researching some people together. There was a popular Mexican American gymnast in the 1970s named Tracee Talavera, but she didn't get to compete in the Olympics because the year she was eligible was the same year the United States boycotted the games—the Olympics were being held in Moscow, and the United States was opposed to the Soviet Union's invasion of Afghanistan, so our president decided our athletes wouldn't go. I felt bad when I heard about that: she'd had all this talent, and she never got the same chance I had. Imagine how many young Latinas she could have inspired! I was also aware of Annia Hatch, who'd won the World Championships for Cuba in 1996. But in our country and in our generation, there are only Kyla Ross and me. Kyla has a Puerto Rican grandparent, and I am fully Puerto Rican American. I read somewhere that less than 4 percent of girls participating in gymnastics in the United States are Hispanic. If you're Latina and you're out there reading this, and you have an interest in gymnastics or any other sport, and you want to go to the Olympics someday—I promise you, it's possible! I am living proof of that. And by the way, the Final Five will be remembered for many things, but one of the greatest attributes is that we are an incredibly diverse team! I'm so glad to be a role model for young Latinas everywhere, especially now that I know there have been so few of us. I take being a role model very seriously, and when you participate in something as important and as global as the Olympics, you have to remember that you're representing yourself, your family, your heritage, your community, and your country—and you have to act accordingly.

For me, the whole homecoming celebration, the stories about my family, friends, and neighbors watching together, and the realization that I could be inspiring future Latina gymnasts were all very humbling and gratifying. And in many ways, it was all very well timed, too, because it kept things real and in perspective as I headed out to take a victory lap around the country and to appear on some of my favorite shows.

THE FINAL
STRETCH

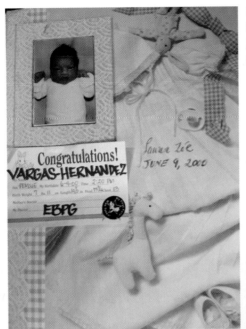

I was born on June 9, 2000, at St. Peter's University Hospital in New Jersey. My mom says I brought joy to the family.

Me, under a year old, apple picking with Mom at Delicious Orchards in New Jersey. I'm sure I was a big help.

My siblings, Marcus and Jelysa, holding me for the first time right after I was born.

Pumpkin picking!

Mugging for the camera—very typical—while camping with the family in Maryland in 2005.

Me at six years old, at my first-ever competition as a gymnast—on a noncompetitive level, but still! So proud.

I love my dad.

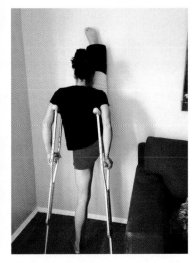

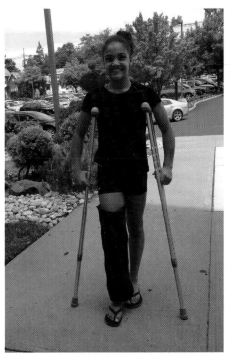

Here's that photo I told you about: The day after surgery in June 2014, after I had torn my patella tendon and had a dislocated kneecap and bruised MCL. I was determined to get better and get back to gymnastics.

On my way to physical therapy with my knee brace, six weeks after surgery.

More recovery: doing physical therapy and getting myself back on track. This was so hard, but with support from my family, I kept going.

I made it to Rio! The Summer Olympic Games, 2016.

The individual balance beam routine that won me silver on August 15, 2016. These moments are so cool to see from the outside.

John Cheng

From my silver medal–winning individual beam routine.

John Cheng

My silver medal ceremony. I was so, so proud of everything I'd accomplished and of how hard I'd worked toward that moment!

I loved every moment of being in Rio. It was amazing to be in the Olympic Village with so many spectacular athletes from around the world.

John Cheng

The Final Five during our team competition gold medal ceremony on August 9, 2016. I love all these girls so much, and I know we'll always share something special. Left to right: Simone Biles, Gabby Douglas, me, Madison Kocian, and Aly Raisman.

August 23, 2016: backstage at *The Tonight Show Starring Jimmy Fallon* with my whole family—can you believe it? Because honestly, I still can't.

Me and my siblings heading to the VMAs in New York City on August 28, 2016—it was my first time seeing my brother and sister after the Olympics. I'll always remember that night and be grateful for their incredible support.

At a Yankees game with my family after the Olympics. Being around them is fun and perfect, and I love getting to come home to them.

Before filming *Good Day New York* right after the Olympics ended. Coming home was such a whirlwind!

Right before my very first competition on *Dancing with the Stars*, September 12, 2016! What a change from gymnastics competitions.

September 3, 2016: I threw out the first pitch at the Mets game, and they gave me the jersey! This was an incredible moment for me.

The day we announced that I would be appearing on *Dancing with the Stars* and that I would partner with Val Chmerkovskiy. We had an AMAZING journey.

At the VMAs with four of the Final Five on August 28, 2016—better known as THE NIGHT I MET BEYONCÉ.

This was October 3, 2016, the night of my first set of perfect 10s on *Dancing with the Stars*. I wasn't expecting that score at all, but Val and I had worked so hard, and it felt wonderful.

Dreams do come true! What an amazing journey and what a special moment. And the very best partner I could've ever asked for—thanks, Val!!!

With Big Bird during my appearance on *Sesame Street*. It was a special treat, and one I'll remember forever.

CHAPTER 16

THE OLYMPICS ARE SUCH AN IMPORTANT COMPE-
tition that, when you're there, you have to tune out
literally everything else. You can't even embrace the fact
that you're a part of this incredible event—it could scare
you and set your mind off the very thing you're there to
do. It's like your feelings are on time delay, so that only
when the craziness dies down can you finally look back
at the amazing experience you had and see it for the
blessing it is. You realize that so few people will ever have
this same opportunity, which connects you even more to
your teammates and your coaches.

Now, what happens *after*, during the post-Olympics

stretch when you're touring the country to share your pride with the nation—that is very different. You're hyperaware of everything that's happening to you as it's happening. At every single event you have at least one *pinch me—is this real?* moment. You planned to compete in the Olympics your whole life, but you really never planned to meet and be celebrated by all your favorite musical artists, actors, comedians, and state leaders!

One of the most amazing things we got to do as we took that victory lap was meet the president and First Lady. Our minute in the spotlight with POTUS and FLOTUS was very funny. They were so humble; it was one of my favorite parts about meeting them. Before either of them entered the room, we all had to place our phones on a table—I guess the rule is no selfies with the First Family. We got to ask Mrs. Obama's staff a bunch of questions before she arrived, and they told us that whenever they take video of her, first she looks down at the floor for the white tape that tells her where to stand for the cameras. At first we thought they were kidding. After all, she's done this a trillion times! But they weren't. Apparently it's a habit of hers. So Simone and Maddy were standing on the left while Aly and I were on the right when the First Lady came in and greeted us. We were super excited to meet her. She was as warm and friendly as we expected her to be, and her smile was so inviting.

But before we shook her hand, she did what her staff predicted she would do: she looked for the white tape and took her place. I don't know why I thought that was so hysterical, but it made me laugh. I guess it reminded me of having to unconsciously check the out-of-bounds lines before beginning my floor routines. I thought it was the funniest thing.

The president wasn't supposed to join us at first, but he said he was such a big fan that he and Vice President Biden just had to stop by and say hello. He pretended to do a few splits with the team, and then we jokingly asked if he would adopt us. Imagine us jumping on the mattresses in the Lincoln Bedroom or spinning on the chair behind his desk in the Oval Office!

Before going to the White House, we were on *The Tonight Show Starring Jimmy Fallon*, which was another awesome experience. We kept thinking, *This is insane!* But even though we were nervous and knew what a big deal it was, we were still able to take it all in and enjoy it. We played a game called Hungry Hungry Humans, which was a riff on the children's game Hungry Hungry Hippos. We had to lie on our stomachs on these moving boards. I was paired with Aly, and she had to grab my ankles and steer me back and forth so I could grab as many loose basketballs as possible and put them in my bucket. The team with the most basketballs in the end won. It was really funny—and a little shocking—to see how competitive we could be. We were so aggressive! It wasn't at all the dignified way we compete in gymnastics. We were definitely going for gold at all costs.

At the VMAs in late August, we had the biggest OMG moment of all. We were there to present the award for best female video. When we opened the envelope with the winner's name on it and saw Beyoncé's, we were thrilled. We waited a minute, and when no one came up to receive the award we thought, *Oh, maybe she's not here.* None of us had seen her arrive earlier, nor had we gotten a glimpse of her in the audience—believe me, we looked! So we thought someone else might be accepting it on her behalf. But that's when we turned and saw her walking up the stairs toward us. We were stunned. We looked at each other like it was Christmas and we'd just gotten the coolest present ever. *Beyoncé was standing there in front of us!* I kept looking at the audience with an expression that said, *Are you catching this?* We each hugged her, and I don't know about the others, but I melted when she put her arms around me. I think we floated offstage after that. I don't usually get flustered when I meet famous people. I'm pretty calm and able to talk to them. I only freak out after they leave. But I have to admit I was very starstruck that night.

Kim and Kanye were there, too, which was fun. Kanye

is an artist both Marcus and I like. When I met him I said, "Wow, your music is amazing. I listen to your albums all the time and think you're a genius!" I made him smile, and that's something he is definitely not known for doing a lot. People joke on Twitter all the time that if you take a rare photo with Kanye smiling, you should report it for good luck. I thought it was hilarious that I got him to look happy. I told Marcus I'm going to have good luck for the rest of my life because Kanye smiled at me. And then, when I asked to take a picture with him, what do you think he did? He said, "Okay, yeah. Sure. No problem," and then he made a super-serious face! I couldn't help but use his own lyrics for the photo caption on Twitter. It read, *I love Kanye more than Kanye loves Kanye!* The truth is, seeing him smile made me love him just a little bit more than I used to.

From there, the fun continued for Simone, Aly, Gabby, Maddy, and me.

Unfortunately, Gabby couldn't join us the night we saw *Hamilton*, but the rest of us went with a few of our coaches and had a great time. I'd never seen a musical live before, so I have nothing to compare it to, but everyone tells me that this is one of the all-time best, and I sensed that without even knowing it for sure. It was pure art and poetry. Basically, it's American history set to rap, and as I mentioned before, I've grown to like history a lot. It was an *amazing* play. I'd really like to see it again to catch any details I might have missed, and maybe to sing along now that the lyrics keep swirling around in my head.

Those are just a few of the highlights from the best summer of my life. But the fall of 2016 did not disappoint, either!

TOUR DE FORCE

CHAPTER 17

FROM SEPTEMBER THROUGH NOVEMBER 2016, IT was time to stop being such fangirls ourselves and start getting out there to meet and entertain our own fans.

We traveled as part of the AEG/USAG's Kellogg's Tour of Gymnastics Champions, which stopped in thirty-six cities. Not only were the Final Five featured in the show, but members of the 2016 men's Olympic and World gymnastics teams starred in it, too. Chris Brooks, Jake Dalton, Danell Leyva, Donothan Bailey, Marvin Kimble, C. J. Maestas, Sam Mikulak, Alex Naddour, Eddie Penev, Donnell Whittenburg, and Brandon Wynn were all there. We were also joined by female Olympic champions

Nastia Liukin, Shawn Johnson, and Jordyn Wieber. I love all three of them. Shawn, as you well know, was one of my earliest inspirations! Few people know this, but when I was going through that rough patch just before the Olympic Trials, I had a phone call with her and she really helped me through it. She told me how she stressed the same exact way and how she just had to work hard to push through. Knowing she'd had those same feelings and still persevered boosted my confidence. In many ways, she, Nastia, and Aly also emboldened me to go on *Dancing with the Stars*. Shawn also won the Mirror Ball Trophy the year she competed, and both Nastia and Aly kicked it on the show, too.

And if that isn't enough talent on one stage, some of the most amazing rhythmic and trampoline artists I've ever seen were in the tour show, too, including Logan Dooley and Nicole Ahsinger. Athlete Laura Zeng was also there, as were members of the first US rhythmic gymnastics group to qualify at the Olympics: Alisa Kano, Natalie McGiffert, Jennifer Rokhman, Monica Rokhman, and Kristie Shaldybin. And World acrobatic gymnasts Tiffani Williams and Axl Osborne performed as well. If you've never watched rhythmic gymnastics, you have to! It combines different forms of dance with gymnastics, working in all kinds of hoops, rings, ribbons, and different apparatus as well. It's so theatrical—you'll love it.

Occasionally MyKayla Skinner, Ragan Smith, or Ashton Locklear would fill in for me or for one of the other gymnasts when there were scheduling conflicts. They, of course, were the phenomenal alternates on our Olympic team. They have a ton of talent individually and collectively. Mary Sanders, a former Olympian in rhythmic gymnastics and one of the creative directors of the tour, also substituted for girls who couldn't make some of the tour dates. There were so many cool people floating in and out of practices and performances all the time, it was crazy.

The tour was like a big welcome-home party for all of us. Everywhere we went, we felt the affection of people who'd watched us in the Olympics or followed us as we competed nationally and internationally throughout the year. The audience was always filled with kids who eat, sleep, and drink gymnastics almost as much as we do. And of course there were those who came even though they themselves had never been on a balance beam or vault in their lives, just because they love to watch gymnastics. When we spoke to the young gymnasts, we found out that many are in their school gymnastics program or are taking local recreational classes. There were even some who are competing at the elite level. Many of the amazing fans who came to see us were joined by their coaches and moms. You can't imagine how much of a community effort it is to raise an athletic child, so it was nice to see them all enjoying an evening out together. They reminded me of me and my MG Elite teammates when we had a chance to unwind with each other after workouts or meets. We always laughed a lot and had such a good time in each other's company. Also, whenever these fans would ask for a picture or an autograph, I thought back to how I felt when I met some of my favorite gymnasts for the first time. I wanted to make these kids feel the same way some of my idols had made me feel. You could see in their eyes how much they love this sport, and I want them to have that look forever.

One time on tour, we did have a spectator who was not like all the others. I couldn't believe it, but musician Tori Kelly showed up! I think that was the time I lost any coolness left in me. Tori is one of my favorite singers in the world. She is such a humble person, and her songs are always so inspiring. She's been my role model for a long time. And her visit was a total surprise. She drove two hours to be there that night, and I can't tell you how much meeting her meant to me. It turned out she's almost as big a fan of me as I am of her! If you don't have a positive role model like her in your life, get one. She reminds me to stay real every day.

At each venue, Kellogg's set up a Fitness and Nutrition Zone so kids could learn about strength, flexibility, and cardio as well as about the importance of eating healthy foods. It was cool because they handed out cereal boxes with our pictures on them! When we're training, our bodies take a pounding. The workouts on an elite level are so strenuous, you need to eat foods that will fuel you, curb any inflammation you might have, and help tweak and tone your muscles, too. I'm not saying that at our fans' ages or skill levels they need to eat like us, but learning to make healthy choices and to provide consistent self-care will give them an advantage later on, whether they compete or just exercise for themselves. In addition to eating well, I think they should hydrate as much as possible and get enough sleep. As you know, I'm all about making sure you're treating yourself well and giving your mind, body, and spirit everything they need to flourish.

My only regret from the tour was that I didn't have more time in each city to explore the local sights. I had never been to most of these places before. But we kept moving so that we could perform in front of as many people in as many cities as possible. The weeks went by so quickly. How we got from Duluth, Georgia, to Spokane, Washington, is a bit of a blur. But even if we didn't stay long in each city, the view from the tour bus window was beautiful a lot of the time. I think everyone should take a cross-country trip at some point. The landscape is so varied and the fall colors were gorgeous.

Of course, one of the best parts of the tour were the antics on the bus rides between cities. We would talk, giggle, play music, and jam out together, or do all of the above at the same time. Around the end of October, we started watching a lot of scary movies—it must have been a Halloween thing. That's when we'd all just huddle up on the couch together under a blanket and scream. I felt sorry for the bus driver!

Then there would be hours at a time when you wouldn't hear a peep from anyone because we were all sound asleep.

Simone and I were on a different bus than Maddy, Aly, and Gabby, but the fun would continue at the hotel and the venue when the five of us were together again. We really are just like a giant family. And with all the other girls included, it was like one big extended family. You would think that us five had had enough of each other by that point, but we hadn't. I'd miss the fun some nights because I would fly back to LA to do *Dancing with the Stars*, but on those days I would Snapchat with the girls to catch up.

I'm not sure everyone can understand the lasting bond we have. Some people think that although we're still close now, our friendship will probably fade over time. But it's not like that at all. We realize that the adventures we have had, and are still having, are once-in-a-lifetime. I believe that as we grow older we're still going to be close. And when I look at Shawn and Nastia's friendship, I know I'm right. They went to the Olympics together, and the bond formed there is still as strong as ever. The same is true of Aly and Jordyn and their 2012 Olympic teammates.

As my journey has continued, I've learned lasting, important lessons about friendships from several different groups of people in my life.

Back in New Jersey, I was lucky to have friends who have known me since I was practically a baby, because my parents and their parents moved into our neighborhood around the same time. We're all close because we had those early years in common.

At Monmouth Gymnastics and at the Karolyi Ranch, my teammates and I had a special common experience that brought us close together. It took me a while to realize that the girls in my gym were the only ones who could understand the kinds of challenges and stresses I faced, because they faced them, too. If I was having a hard day, they could relate without me having to say much. One day I just realized that they would likely be my closest friends throughout my career and probably throughout my life.

Friendships are built on understanding, and our

common experiences provided that understanding. What makes our bond even stronger is that our common experiences aren't all that common. We exist in a unique world—the world of competitive gymnastics. The way we pushed ourselves throughout our childhoods made our childhoods different than everyone else we know. I've already written a little bit about how special my friendship is with my teammate Jazmyn Foberg because of this understanding. We both had a lot of rough practices and meets together, so we always tried to help each other get through them emotionally and physically.

Seeing so many kids who love gymnastics show up at the tour made me realize how big the world of gymnastics is, but knowing so many amazing athletes and traveling with as many of them as I have during the tour also helped me realize how small a world it is, too. I hope the kids who came out to see the tour enjoyed our performances, and I especially hope that whether they go to the Olympics or not one day, they have the kinds of friendships with other gymnasts that I have enjoyed at every level!

DANCING
ON AIR

CHAPTER 18

THIS WILL PROBABLY COME AS A BIG SURPRISE, but it's my dad who's most responsible for me joining the cast of *Dancing with the Stars*. My agent, Sheryl Shade, brought me the opportunity, and Aly's, Nastia's, and Shawn's performances on the show attracted me to it as well—but it was my father who first put the idea in my head.

Out of everyone in my family, my dad is the biggest music lover of all. He and my mom are always dancing together at parties, and he jokes that my rhythm is so good because it runs in his family. About eight years ago, we all started watching *DWTS* together. At first, my dad wasn't thrilled about joining us, because the show airs at the same time as *Monday Night Football* and he's a huge football fan. But he always puts his kids first, so he gave it a try. Before long he was just as addicted as the rest of us. Then one evening when we were watching, he turned to me and said, "You know, sweetie, you're going to be on that show someday, too." I gave him a side eye and said, "Sure, Dad. Whatever you say." But the seed of an idea had been planted. . . .

All those years later, when they asked me during the Olympics to be on the show, I was ecstatic. Of all the gymnastics events, floor is the only one where I'm able to dance and really let my personality shine. When you're doing a bars or beam routine, you're basically just showcasing skills; you can't show much personality. And the audience isn't even able to see how happy I am to be doing it. But during my floor exercise, I get to flaunt how joyful I am. I don't ever feel like I have to hide anything from the judges or the crowd. That's initially how I knew I could successfully make the leap from gymnastics to dance.

Aside from my early-childhood ballet class—where I was focused more on my late-afternoon snack than on technique—and the few ballet classes I took during National Team Training Camps in Texas, I'd never actually had any real dance experience. I quickly learned that my elite training was nothing compared to what I would go through while rehearsing for *Dancing with the Stars*! When you watch the show, it's easy to see it as just two people gliding across the floor. Sometimes you might note that one dance is extremely powerful or that another is upbeat and a lot of fun—but besides that, you likely don't see all the footwork and passion that goes into making it look easy, natural, elegant, and organic. It's hard to get people to understand that it's so much more difficult to do than it looks.

The first week I started rehearsals and had to learn a new dance, I found it mind-blowing. I only did well because I had such a generous dance partner. The day I met Val Chmerkovskiy was kind of funny. A lot of people think I live this sophisticated life because I've competed in international events and I've gone to the Olympics and I've toured all over the United States. But as many of you found out later on in the show when I told Val I'd never been to the prom, I really didn't get to do a lot of things normal teens get to do. I had been so devoted to gymnastics for so long, there were a lot of "firsts" I missed out on. And that was really apparent the day Val walked into the gym where I was practicing for the Kellogg's Tour. No one had told me yet who my dance partner would be. I think they wanted it to be a surprise. When he walked in, all I could think was, *Oh my gosh, this is crazy. It's already starting.*

Almost immediately Val wanted to see what I could do, so he grabbed my hand and began dancing with me. I could barely concentrate on the dance, because here was this grown man touching my hand and swinging me around. It felt so weird—which I totally couldn't say to him or to anyone else at the time. But one of the things Val emphasized with me throughout our time together is the value of feeling your emotions and communicating them. That was probably the single most important skill that came out of my experience on *Dancing with the Stars*. I struggled with communication a lot in the first few rehearsals, as we talked about in the video packages. I love to write and my family is big on talking things out with each other so we could remain close as a family, so I had actually imagined that I was a good communicator before all this. But there was a level of professional communication I hadn't had a chance to fully develop. The way you work with your partner on *DWTS* is very different from the way you work with your coach in elite gymnastics. There's an expression in gymnastics we all laugh at because it's pretty close to the truth: "If your coach tells you to land on your neck, you land on your neck." Of course, no coach will ever ask you to do that, but the saying means that the coach knows what's best for you, and they will push you as hard as they have to in order to get the best results. Your job is to bend to what they're asking you to do until you can do it over and over again and you can do it better than anyone else. By contrast, Val's style of communication, and the style of communication between dance partners, is a real give-and-take. You have to tell the other person when something is off or else it will show in the final dance. It's about being in sync with each other at all times. And you can't be in sync if you don't know what the other person is feeling emotionally and physically. So Val repeatedly encouraged me to tell him whenever I was uncomfortable with something. If I couldn't get a step right or if I became frustrated with myself and didn't share the reason, he would insist that I express what was going on inside my head. At which point I had a breakthrough: in dance you don't just deal with it; you can actually address the challenge and either work through it together or change the steps to effectively reflect the emotion the dance requires.

Exercising my voice with Val was like training a muscle. But I'm happy to say that we worked on it and I was much better by the end of the season! Just spending time together and getting to know each other really helped.

Because I was on the Kellogg's Tour at the same time I was on *DWTS*, I would travel to each city by bus with my teammates, and Val would fly to the city where I was performing each week to meet me. The day I arrived in a new city I would have off from *DWTS* practice because traveling is exhausting and I usually had to perform gymnastics that same night. The next morning Val and I would rehearse, and later that night I would perform gymnastics again. Sometimes he flew back to LA and I would meet him there later, while other times I flew with him. During those flights we got to know each other better, but it was funny how our conversations would always drift back to our routine.

To be a good communicator you also have to be a good observer, and Val really has that skill. One day, when we were in Seattle, we ended practice early and left the dance studio. He took me to this famous open-air fish market called Pike Place. When you buy fish there, the vendors throw it up in the air before they wrap it and they play all these games the way old-time fishmongers did. It's very entertaining. We also walked through a produce market where we bought fresh fruit, and then we walked through this cute neighborhood. I was so moved that he took the time to do that, because he could obviously see that I didn't get to go out often. It was just nice to be able to walk around freely. I've spent so much of my life in a gym, even my parents had to make sure that I got out for a concert, some ice cream, some retail therapy with my sister, or a hangout with my brother at the local

Wawa. I'm happy Val had the same urge to make time for a break. I'm not sure if he knows how much it meant to me to get away from everything and go exploring for a change. It was so thoughtful of him—I'm definitely going to remember that.

TRIPLE 10s

CHAPTER 19

ONE SIGN I WAS IMPROVING MY COMMUNICATION skills was that Val and I joked around with each other a lot more as the season progressed. Another sign was that I was dancing better than I ever had before, thanks to him.

One of the highlights of being on *Dancing with the Stars* was earning a perfect 10 on Val's and my jazz performance to the tune of Michael Jackson's "The Way You Make Me Feel." It was great for all the obvious reasons: getting that kind of score meant that I was doing a lot of things right and that I was not only beginning to master the techniques of the dance, I was reflecting the *heart* of the dance, too.

Val always says that the steps are secondary: the real success of a dance is how you make people feel when they watch you. So getting perfect 10s across the board was super satisfying, because it meant I had stirred some real and vibrant emotions in the audience. As the title suggests, the song is about the way someone makes you feel, so my whole goal that week was to make the audience really *feel* something. Succeeding at that was a real breakthrough for me.

It may sound surprising, but dance is as much about acting as it is about rhythm and physical agility. In every dance we were telling a story, and whatever character I played had to help drive that story emotionally. I already loved acting, but I realized that in order to improve my dancing, I also had to improve my acting.

It was easy enough for me to get into character during the first few weeks. For the cha-cha I hooked into how much both music and dance are a part of my Latin heritage, and I let that inspire my character. In the next week, we danced the jive, which is very fast and playful. I had to get into a very different mind-set, but because we used the theme from *Duck Tales*, I thought about how animation works and I made all my character choices very big. I almost couldn't believe it when Julianne Hough called me Disney's Beyoncé.

But rehearsals the next week weren't as magical for me. I struggled with the acting element of the tango. Val kept trying to get me to feel what the character in that dance would feel so that my character could connect better with his character. The problem was that I've never had a boyfriend, so I've never experienced a breakup, either. It's frustrating to have to channel feelings you've never had, so I realized I had to focus on *acting* them more than *channeling* them. To help me out, Val kept trying to think of movies that could trigger the feeling of loss my character was supposed to feel. He talked about *The Notebook*, which helped a little, but then he made me laugh when he suggested that I think about how the dad in *Finding Nemo* must have felt when he lost his son—I got it on some level, but I've also never been a parent!

As I told Ellen DeGeneres when we were on her show, it was a lightbulb moment right before we went onstage that night that kind of saved me. To help me at least make the right gesture during the tango, I dramatized smelling a quesadilla. All in one connected sequence, I threw my head and right shoulder back, closed my eyes, and drew a deep breath as a smile crossed my face. Anyone would have thought I was thinking about my star-crossed lover, but I was really anticipating taking a bite of one of my favorite foods. Hey, whatever works!

The very next week when I was learning the steps to the jazz dance and I found that it was easier channeling the emotion of my character than getting all the steps down, I felt a real sense of accomplishment. The perfect 10s were confirmation that I'd gotten over that acting hurdle I'd found so tough the week before.

There were other weeks when I had to try to imagine certain experiences rather than channel them, but by then Val and I were communicating so well that it was way easier. The particular week that comes to mind was when the dances were inspired by different decades. Our dance that time was set in the 1960s, *well* before I was born, so Val and I didn't dance at all during the first rehearsal. Instead we researched all the things that happened to make the sixties so rebellious. And when Val discovered that I had never been to the prom because I was homeschooled, he also helped create that experience for me. Instead of trying to draw from experiences I hadn't had yet, I was learning how to make imagined experiences more real to me. I was getting a dancing, acting, and life lesson all at one time!

I learn by watching, so I was always engrossed when the other couples danced. They all had their inspired moments, but one couple I consistently enjoyed was James Hinchcliffe and Sharna Burgess. I think it was because

James really did make acting such a seamless part of his performance. The same week I did the prom dance, I was in awe as I watched him and Sharna do the jitterbug. I loved every facial expression and body gesture he made. Following his characters' stories was always so much fun.

In addition to learning the acting aspect of dance, I also had to learn to process the judges' critiques in a meaningful way. The tricky thing about the show is that you move on to a new style of dance every week, so it can be difficult to show them that you understood and applied their comments from the previous week. We would put so much effort into our dances that the moment I stood next to cohost Tom Bergeron to hear the judges' feedback was always nerve-racking. My heart would pound so loudly every time, I was sure the mic would pick it up! During the first week when I danced the cha-cha, I was happy judge Carrie Ann Inaba sensed I was hungering to learn ballroom dancing. I didn't want to squander the opportunity to learn from Val and the judges by relying only on my gymnastics background, so it was good that my eagerness showed. Then judge Julianne Hough gave me specific advice. I had seen her dance on the show before, so I knew what she said in terms of technique would help. She was pleased with my arm and leg action, but both she and judge Bruno Tonioli thought I needed to work on loosening up my hips.

I laughed to myself because there had been many times before a gymnastics competition when I heard, "Oh no, she can't move her hips like that." Then I would have to go back and change up my routine so it was tamer. Now I was hearing the complete opposite. I had to move my hips *more*! Honestly, at first it was uncomfortable, because I'd put my hips away for so long. After that, I worked hard to keep my dance performances free of the parts of my gymnastics training that didn't belong. That was definitely the case when I danced the tango. Because my connection to my partner had to be evident during that dance, I had to make sure no one could detect that in gymnastics I always danced solo!

There was one time, however, that I wished my gymnastics story had been better understood and that the feedback from the judges had been different. It was the week after we had scored triple 10s with our jazz dance, so the pressure was on to outdo ourselves. To make matters more complicated, we were dancing the *paso doble*. My first reaction was *the paso what?* I had never heard of it before. My feet were tired from wearing heels, and even icing my toes the way Shawn and Nastia had suggested wasn't helping with the soreness.

The *paso doble*, as it turned out, was a very intense

dance. I had to get in touch with feelings from some of the most serious events in my life for my character to convey the right emotions. So I focused on all the trials I'd had in the gym when I was fighting my way back from injury in the two years leading up to the Olympics. The dance began with me alone in a tight box. It was supposed to evoke the claustrophobic feelings I'd felt during that rough period: I could never take time off, and even if my family went on vacation, I couldn't go with them because I had to train. The box symbolized how lonely it had been at times, but in the end I pushed through the walls and exploded onto the floor. It was a metaphor for the way I felt about my return from Rio and being on *Dancing with the Stars*; it reflected how much I was enjoying myself and how liberated I was feeling because of dance. So when the judges didn't think it was a necessary part of the dance, I silently disagreed. They explained how the *paso doble* is about having a connection with your partner. For this reason, they thought starting off by myself was contrary to the distinct style of the dance. But I felt that the dance we did showed a deep connection between our characters. My character had to have a breakthrough before she could unite with Val's character, and when she did, that breakthrough made their connection that much more powerful. The next day I came into rehearsal with

Val and said, "What did they mean, we needed more connection? I thought we had a lot of connection!" He just laughed and said he thought the dance had been perfect even if the judges didn't think so. He told me not only that it was amazing but also that he was very proud of me. Honestly, it meant more to me that Val was proud than another round of straight 10s would have. I was on the show to grow and learn, and I felt that was exactly what I was doing. I was glad Val saw that growth, too.

We worked even harder in the weeks that followed. I took a break from the gymnastics tour because I really wanted to look like a professional as we continued to compete. Val is a phenomenal dancer, but he sees being a teacher as more valuable. His students are his legacy. He always says he wants to be sure that I can do everything he teaches me after he's gone from the classroom. I was speechless on Halloween night when he got so emotional. I think he knew I wanted to be the best student. I got emotional, too, when he told cohost Erin Andrews, "My inspiration is to be able to pass my blessings on forward, and I appreciate the opportunity to be able to inspire young talent like Laurie." And then he added, "In the process, maybe she can change the world."

We got another set of perfect 10s that night. And the truth is, Val did help change my world. I was thrilled beyond words when we won the Mirror Ball Trophy. We earned a combined two-night score of 118 points in the finals—not to mention picking up two more perfect 10s. And I'm even more humbled to be the youngest contestant ever to win *DWTS*!

I couldn't believe the wave of renewed energy that carried me into those last two evenings. On the first night, I loved revisiting our *paso doble* for the redemption round to the tune of "Wicked Ones" by Dorothy. Everything about it just felt right! But it was the freestyle to Ben Rector's "Brand New" where I really let loose and had the most fun. Since Val is like family now, the choice of dancing the samba trio with him and his brother, Maks, to "Megalenha" by Sergio Mendes for our encore on the second night seemed completely natural to me, too. But if you had told me in week one that I'd end the season with a foxtrot and Argentine tango fusion, I'm not sure I would have believed you! I've come such a long way. As we moved to Myon's inspiring "We Are the Ones," I just knew we could win. And we did! It was an especially awesome achievement because we were up against the fiercest of competitors: Sharna and James, who took second place, and Lindsay and Calvin, who took third. Both couples danced their hearts out week after week, so it was an honor to take it to the end with them.

I had so much fun doing the show. It truly impacted my life in so many surprising ways, but honestly, I don't think it's always the Mirror Ball that's the prize. I really believe you win in this contest and every other contest in life the minute you take on and commit to the challenge!

I loved Calvin Johnson's story about why he joined the cast of *DWTS* this season. During an interview with Lisa Salters on ESPN, his sister told the world that she didn't think her brother had rhythm or could dance. If my brother said that about me on TV (and thankfully he never has!), I would want to prove him wrong, too.

When I heard Calvin tell that story, I realized every one of us had come on the show for more than the Mirror Ball Trophy. Most of us were there to challenge ourselves, to push our limits, to apply skills we already had to something new, to inspire our loved ones to keep growing, too, and to write another exciting life chapter. I knew I would learn about dance—what I didn't know was that I'd learn so much about myself. I feel as if I grew as a person every week on the show. I pushed myself to feel a whole range of emotions I didn't know I had, and when I was asked to portray an emotion I couldn't really access, I learned how to imagine how that emotion might feel. (Okay, there were a few I had to flat-out fake!) Yes, there is definitely some acting involved in gymnastics floor exercises, but dancing helped me kick those skills up a few notches. And since then, I've made my formal acting debut. Did you see me counting to five with Grover on *Sesame Street*? Or appearing as myself on *Stuck in the Middle*? I've always dreamed of being in an action-adventure movie, so who knows, maybe I can do that next!

I expected to do my best throughout the whole *DWTS* competition. What I didn't expect was to be so moved every week as I watched all the others do their best, too.

I also expected to laugh a little and have fun with my dance partner. I didn't expect to laugh all the time! And I definitely didn't expect to confess to the judges or to Ellen DeGeneres that I still sleep with my teddy bear! By the way, being on Ellen's show was insane. She is as funny off camera as she is on. When Val and I entered the building where the show is filmed, she was in the lobby playing Ping-Pong! I asked her and the crew if this was an everyday thing, and they said, "Absolutely!" So I couldn't help myself. I blurted out, "Ellen, if you play Ping-Pong all the time, why didn't I see you at the Olympics?" She just smiled and said, "You did. I was there. I was just in a different building." I thought she was hilarious!

BEYOND THE MIRROR BALL TROPHY

CHAPTER 20

ULTIMATELY, THIS IS THE OVERRIDING MESSAGE I want you to take away from my story: *You win whenever you commit to something, because you can't experience growth without even trying.*

Many years ago I found a sport I absolutely love to do. I pursued gymnastics with my whole heart. I gave it all the energy, focus, and determination I possibly could. There were disappointing days. There were even times when either my body or my spirit seriously entertained the notion of quitting. But I kept going. By now you know that I can't imagine what my life would be like if I hadn't taken a chance and committed to those challenges.

. . .

A little before the Olympics began and certainly after the Olympics ended, I had to think about setting some new goals. It's always hard to do that when you've been concentrating on one mission for such a long time. I asked myself some important questions: Would I go to college and compete on the NCAA level? Or would I go pro? Would I travel on the Kellogg's Tour and be away from my family for even longer stretches of time than usual? Would I join *Dancing with the Stars* to learn and exercise some new skills?

Sometimes setting goals and making choices can seem overwhelming, so I decided to take each question one by one. I gave myself enough time to weigh the pros and the cons, but not too much time that I lost my momentum. I decided to go pro because the opportunities coming my way were just too exciting to pass up. They were chances that might not come my way again, and I believed that all of them offered me an opportunity to grow and learn. Since my family and I really do value education, I also knew that I could return to school for a higher degree at any time in the future.

I also decided to tour with Kellogg's and had an incredibly fun time. And of course, I competed on (and won!) *Dancing with the Stars* and joined their national tour as well. Plus, as part of my Olympic dream coming true, I've been privileged to endorse leotard brand GK, Nike, and P&G.

After each success 1 had with those ventures, it seemed like even more offers rolled in. So you see how making an effort just helps more good things happen? I am lucky to have my family and other professional people around me to help me make wise decisions, but I'm also listening to my heart as I have always done—it seems to know what's best a lot of the time.

Not all my goals from here on out will be as big as going to the Olympics, but I like having expectations and meeting them. It's a great way to make sure you are getting the most out of your life.

Some of you may already have big goals that you are working toward. Some of you may have smaller goals. And a few of you may still be in search of at least one good one to pursue. Wherever you are on that spectrum, I can't encourage you enough to think about, reach for, and achieve your dreams. The feeling is like nothing else in the world. And when you do succeed, don't be afraid to hit reset and dare to dream again! That's what I'm doing, and what I hope you do, too.

YOUR TURN

When I decided to go pro, my agent and friend, Sheryl Shade, gave me a journal. She told me to write in it every day. She said it would be important to remember all the things that were happening in my life at any given moment for when I wanted to tell my children or my grandchildren about them, for when I just wanted to refresh my own memory, or for when I eventually wanted to write about my story. She also told me not only to look back but to look ahead: the journal was where I could make lists of all the things I wanted to do in the future.

I want to pass on that inspiration to you. Think of the next few pages as your *possibility pages*. Start writing some goals you'd like to reach today, tomorrow, this year, a few years from now. They can be large or small. And as you make your list, remember the words I wrote at the start of this book: *You got this!*

LAURIE'S OFFICIAL RECORDS

National Competition Results

2016 US Olympic Team Trials, San Jose, California (Sr. Division)

1st Balance Beam; 2nd All-Around; 3rd Floor Exercise; 4th Vault; 7th Uneven Bars

2016 P&G Championships, St. Louis, Missouri (Sr. Division)

3rd All-Around, Uneven Bars, Balance Beam, Floor Exercise (Tie)

2016 Secret US Classic, Hartford, Connecticut (Sr. Division)
4th Uneven Bars

2015 P&G Championships, Indianapolis, Indiana (Jr. Division)
1st All-Around, Uneven Bars; 2nd Floor Exercise; 3rd Vault (Tie), Balance Beam

2015 Secret US Classic, Chicago, Illinois (Jr. Division)
1st All-Around, Vault, Uneven Bars; 3rd Balance Beam, Floor Exercise (Tie)

2013 P&G Championships, Hartford, Connecticut (Jr. Division)
2nd All-Around, Uneven Bars, Floor Exercise; 3rd Balance Beam (Tie); 5th Vault

2013 Secret US Classic, Chicago, Illinois (Jr. Division)
1st Floor Exercise; 6th All-Around; 8th Vault, Uneven Bars

2013 American Classics, Huntsville, Texas (Jr. Division)
1st Floor Exercise; 2nd All-Around; 3rd Vault, Balance Beam; 7th Uneven Bars

2013 Parkettes Invitational, Allentown, Pennsylvania (Jr. Division)
1st Uneven Bars, Balance Beam, Floor Exercise, All-Around; 3rd Vault

2012 Secret US Classic, Chicago, Illinois (Jr. Division)
6th Floor Exercise; 7th Balance Beam

International Competition Results
2016 Olympic Games, Rio de Janeiro, Brazil
1st Team; 2nd Balance Beam

2016 Pacific Rim Championships, Everett, Washington (Sr. Division)
1st Team

2016 Jesolo Trophy, Jesolo, Italy (Sr. Division)
1st Team, Balance Beam; 2nd Vault; 3rd All-Around

2015 Junior Japan International, Yokohama, Japan
1st All-Around, Vault, Floor Exercise; 2nd Uneven Bars, Balance Beam

2015 Jesolo Trophy, Jesolo, Italy (Jr. Division)
1st Team, All-Around, Uneven Bars, Floor Exercise

2013 International Junior Mexican Cup, Acapulco, Mexico
1st Team; 2nd All-Around

2013 International Junior Gymnastics Competition, Yokohama, Japan (Jr. Division)
3rd All-Around, Vault; 4th Floor Exercise; 6th Balance
Beam

GLOSSARY OF GYMNASTICS TERMS

AERIAL

A stunt in which the gymnast turns completely over in the air without touching the apparatus with his or her hands.

ALL-AROUND

A category of gymnastics that includes all the events. The all-around champion of an event earns the highest total score from all events combined.

AMPLITUDE

The height or degree of execution of a movement. In general, the higher the salto or the more breathtaking the movement, the better the amplitude and the score.

APPARATUS

One of the various pieces of equipment used in gymnastics competitions.

ARCH POSITION

The body is curved backward.

BACK-IN, FULL-OUT

A double salto with a full twist (the complete twist performed during the second salto).

CODE OF POINTS

The official FIG rulebook for judging gymnastics skills.

COMPOSITION

The structure of a gymnastics routine. Each individual movement or skill is a building block; the arrangement of the moves in the exercise is called the composition of the routine.

DEDUCTION

Points taken off a gymnast's score for errors. Most deductions are predetermined, such as a 0.8 deduction for a fall from an apparatus or a 0.1 deduction for stepping out of bounds on the floor exercise.

DISMOUNT

To leave an apparatus at the end of a routine; usually done with a difficult twist or salto.

EXECUTION

The performance of a routine. Form, style, and technique used to complete the skills constitute the level of execution of an exercise. Bent knees, poor toe point, and an arched or loosely held body position are all examples of poor execution.

FIG

The International Gymnastics Federation—which is known officially in the French, *Fédération Internationale de Gymnastique*, because its headquarters are in Switzerland—is recognized by the International Olympic Committee and is responsible for the governance of the sport of gymnastics on the international level.

FLEXIBILITY

The range of motion through which a body part can move without feeling pain.

FLIC-FLAC

Also known as a flip-flop or back handspring. Take off on one or two feet, jump backward onto hands, and land on feet. This element is used in a majority of tumbling passes on the floor exercise. It's also used a great deal on the balance beam.

FULL-IN, BACK-OUT

A double salto with a full twist (the complete twist performed during the first salto).

GAYLORD

On high bar, a front giant into a one-and-one-half front salto over the bar to regrasp. First done by US gymnast Mitch Gaylord.

GIANT

A swing in which the body is fully extended and moving through a 360-degree rotation around the bar.

HALF-IN, HALF-OUT

A double salto with a half twist on the first salto and a half twist on the second salto.

HANDSPRING

Springing off the hands by putting the weight on the arms and using a strong push from the shoulders; can be done either forward or backward; usually a linking movement.

KIP

Movement from a position below the equipment to a position above, usually on the uneven bars, parallel bars, or high bar.

LAYOUT POSITION

A stretched body position.

OLYMPIC ORDER

The international competition order that is decided by the FIG. Olympic order for women is vault, uneven bars, balance beam, and floor exercise. Men compete in the following order: floor exercise, pommel horse, still rings, vault, parallel bars, and horizontal bar. Olympic order for rhythmic gymnasts is rope, hoop, ball, clubs, and ribbon.

PIKE POSITION

Body bent forward more than ninety degrees at the hips while the legs are kept straight.

PIROUETTE

Changing direction or moving in a circular motion by twisting in the handstand position.

RELEASE

Leaving the bar to perform a move before regrasping it.

ROUND-OFF

A dynamic turning movement, with a push-off on one leg, while swinging the legs upward in a fast cartwheel motion into a ninety-degree turn. The leadoff to a number of skills.

ROUTINE

A combination of stunts displaying a full range of skills on one apparatus.

SALTO

Flip or somersault, with the feet coming up over the head and the body rotating around the axis of the waist.

SCISSORS

A combination requirement in a competitive routine on the pommel horse, which combines cuts and undercuts. It begins in a stride support and ends in an opposite stride support.

SEQUENCE

Two or more positions or skills that are performed together, creating a different skill or activity.

"STUCK" LANDING

Slang term used for when a gymnast executes a landing with correct technique and no movement of the feet.

TUCK

A position in which the knees and hips are bent and drawn into the chest; the body is folded at the waist.

TWIST

Not to be confused with a salto, a twist occurs when the gymnast rotates around the body's longitudinal axis, defined by the spine.

VIRTUOSITY

The artistry, or the degree of rhythm and harmony,

displayed while a movement is executed. In general, the more flowing and seamless a series of skills appears to be, the greater the virtuosity and the higher the score.

YURCHENKO VAULT

Named for the Soviet gymnast Natalia Yurchenko, this is a round-off entry onto the board, flic-flac onto the vaulting table, and salto off the vaulting table. The gymnast may twist on the way off.

ACKNOWLEDGMENTS

So many people have helped me throughout my life and career. There may not be enough space on these pages to thank everyone, but if you have cheered for me, encouraged me, and cared for me somewhere along the way, please know there is plenty of space in my heart for you!

I am extremely grateful to my 2016 Olympic teammates, Simone Biles, Gabby Douglas, Madison Kocian, and Aly Raisman, and to our alternates, Ashton Locklear, MyKayla Skinner, and Ragan Smith. Thank you from the bottom of my heart for some of the most amazing memories!

I am also extremely grateful to Marta Karolyi, the

ACKNOWLEDGMENTS

National Team coordinator for USA Gymnastics; Rhonda Faehn, senior vice president of the women's program at USA Gymnastics; Head Coach Aimee Boorman; Coach Mihai Brestyan; Coach Christian Gallardo; Coach Laurent Landi, and, of course, Coach Maggie Haney, who has been my dedicated coach for almost a decade. I can't thank you all enough for your encouragement, support, and trust in me, and our whole team!

Many thanks, too, to the entire USAG organization. Continued gratitude to my awesome medical team, including everyone at USAG's medical office, especially Debbie Van Horn, as well as Dr. David Gentile, Dr. John Fulkerson, Dr. Jidong Sun, Dr. Sunny Shen, Malvin Torralba, Dr. Scott Greenberg, Dr. Michael Lagana, Dr. Olga Belder, Dr. Cavan Brunsden, Dr. Nancy Villa, Dr. James Wolf, Angelo Pollari, and Robert Andrews. You all helped heal me when I was broken. It's good to be whole again.

I wish to thank all my friends at MG Elite and Gymland, including Jazzy, Riley, and Emily; all the gym moms (there are too many of you to thank individually, but you know who you are!); my neighbors, forever friends, and family who were always there for me, particularly Laurie, Al, Emily, and Alyssa Liszewski; Anna, Juan, Paloma, and Shannon Rodriguez; the Robert Christian family; the Mercado and Vargas family; the Pinho family; the

Deserio family; the LaFranca family; the Vigilante family; the Salazar family; the Graulau family; the Foberg family; the Merriweather family; the LosKamp family; the Wilentz family; Chris and Jackie Green; Diana Rios; Grandma Bruny; Grandma Ita; Tio Jose; the Garcia family; Pastor Dan; and Pastor Angelo. You've all had a part in my success.

Special thanks as well to Coach Yuriy Aminov from Monmouth Gymnastics, for his continued encouragement throughout the years.

Lots of xo's to the Plum Leo staff and crew, too—Nicole Midura, John Mytschenko, Gennaro Palladino, Brant Lutska, and the Rizzo family. My years modeling with you gave me so much confidence and even more happy memories!

Deep appreciation also extends to the entire cast of the AEG/USAG's Kellogg's Tour of Gymnastics Champions and the show's amazing staff and crew. Thank you, Shawn Johnson and Nastia Liukin, in particular, for taking me under your wings on the tour and for advising me on *Dancing with the Stars* as well.

I am especially grateful to my awesome *DWTS* partner, Val Chmerkovskiy; all the other pros and contestants on the show; hosts Tom Bergeron and Erin Andrews; as well as all the judges: Carrie Ann Inaba, Len Goodman,

Julianne Hough, and Bruno Tonioli. I have learned so much from you all. I'm thankful, too, for the efforts of the talented designers, crew, and helpful administrative staff. And I am especially grateful to Deena Katz, the show's co-executive producer and head of casting, who saw me at the Olympic Trials and knew then that I should be on the show!

A big shout-out to Lisa Sharkey and my editor, Sara Sargent, at HarperCollins and to my collaborator, Hope Innelli. This book wouldn't be possible without all of your help!

Hugs to my agent, Sheryl Shade, who is doing an amazing job navigating me through this next exciting chapter of my career and life. I am so fortunate to have found such a force of good! Special thanks as well to her associate Shannon Lynch, and to my PMK publicist, Meghan Prophet, for all they do every day.

Huge thanks to all the young gymnasts and dancers who continue to watch and support me, and all the readers who bought this book!

And finally, my never-ending love and gratitude to my family and to God for all the blessings I've received.

ABOUT THE AUTHOR

Laurie Hernandez is an American gymnast, an Olympic gold medalist, and a *Dancing with the Stars* champion. At the 2016 Olympic Games in Rio, Laurie won silver in the individual balance beam competition and secured gold in the team all-around competition.

Laurie started gymnastics at the age of six because she wanted to experience the feeling of flying. She enrolled at Monmouth Gymnastics in New Jersey, where she met her coach, and they became a winning duo. The turning point in Laurie's career came in 2014, when her progress was stalled due to multiple injuries. She returned stronger than ever by becoming the 2015 US junior national champion. Laurie's other career highlights include all-around silver, beam gold, and floor exercise bronze at the 2016 US Olympic Trials and bronze in all-around, floor exercise, beam, and uneven bars at the 2016 P&G National Championships. Laurie is known for her dazzling floor exercise routines and for her grace and artistry on the balance beam. And she has been nicknamed "the Human Emoji" for her outgoing facial expressions.